Room 109

Room 109

The Promise of a Portfolio Classroom

Richard Kent

Boynton/Cook Publishers
HEINEMANN
Portsmouth, NH

Boynton/Cook Publishers, Inc.
A subsidiary of Reed Elsevier Inc.
361 Hanover Street
Portsmouth, NH 03801–3912
Offices and agents throughout the world

Library of Congress Cataloging-in-Publication Data

Kent, Richard Burt.
    Room 109 : the promise of a portfolio classroom / Richard Kent.
      p.   cm.
    Includes bibliographical references.
    ISBN 0-86709-429-X
    1. Portfolios in education—United States—Case studies.
I. Title.
LB1029.P67K45   1997
371.39—dc21   97-15865
                                                  CIP

Editor: *Thomas Newkirk*
Manufacturing: *Louise Richardson*
Cover design: *Barbara Werden*

Printed in the United States of America on acid-free paper
00   99   98   97   DA   1   2   3   4   5   6   7   8   9

For Barbara and Ken,
caretakers and lifegivers.

In celebration of Anne Wood,
dear friend.

In memory of Jon Sassi.

Contents

Acknowledgments

Perhaps *Room 109* began in 1958 when I entered Miss Bessey's kindergarten class at Virginia Elementary School. There, I learned about caring from a thoughtful teacher who always treated my best friend, Tippy, to a bowl of milk at recess.

This book's roots were nourished in Mrs. Puiia's creative writing class in 1971 at Rumford High School. There, as a sixteen-year-old, I was inspired to play with words and to seek new ideas.

In some ways this book has been in the works for generations. The most recent collaborator was my mother, Barbara Burt Kent. In the last years of her life while battling leukemia, she taught homebound students, many of whom were as ill as she. During those days, this fourth-generation teacher taught all of us what it is to live a life of grace.

To each of them and to all the teachers of my life—both in and out of school—I offer my deepest gratitude and respect.

I also wish to thank the following:

- Tom Rowe and Dick Blackman, principals and friends, whose leadership in the newly formed Mountain Valley High School provided an atmosphere of respect and professionalism

- Walter Buotte, Ken Nye, and Howard Johnson, principals of the highest caliber, who shared their vision and friendship

- Dixie Goswami, Michael Armstrong, and the late James Britton of The Bread Loaf School of English for playing vital, perhaps irreplaceable, roles in my learning and teaching life

- Bread Loaf's director, James Maddox, a millworker's son himself, who encouraged my work and supported me during the trying times that public school practitioners often experience

- Linda Worthing and Joe Sassi, of the Mountain Valley Media Center, for supporting my research as well as sharing Jolly Ranchers and conversation when things got hectic

- Kenric Charles, my assistant principal, for support, laughter, and the firm yet gentle hand of leadership

- Burt deFrees, Paula Dupil, Roger Fuller, Kathy Kellogg, Jerry Kiesman, Sue Long, Barbara Trafton, Monica Wood, and JoAnne Zywna for reading portions of this book and commenting with sensitivity and objectivity (special thanks to JoAnne for encouraging a young writer eighteen years ago)

- Jane Holt deFrees and Marjorie Murray Medd, former chairs of the Maine State Board of Education, for friendship and for their unselfish work on behalf of learning in the State of Maine

- Suzie Cary, who offered long-distance E-mail support and friendship almost every day for the past four years

- Janet Allen for pointing me in the right direction and encouraging this book

- Matthew Peterson, a student colleague, who served as my research assistant during the final year of this book's writing

- The Milken Family Foundation, the International Paper Company, and The U.S. Space and Rocket Center for their support of my work and that of America's teachers

- The custodial staff of S.A.D. #43 for summertime serenades and late-night conversations

- My colleagues in S.A.D. #43 for their acts of kindness and for their professionalism

- My niece, Melissa Michaud, a sixth-generation teacher, whose passion, professionalism, and caring give me hope for the future of our vocation

Tom Newkirk, my Heinemann editor, listened and listened. Then, with just the right words, he helped me see what I was saying. As with all effective teachers, Tom taught me to trust myself.

Anne Wood read and edited every page of every draft of this book. She cheerfully took nine P.M. "What-does-this-sound-like?" phone calls and offered encouragement and insight. This book is one more legacy for this teacher of teachers.

The members of my family—Allen, Barbara, Ken, Pam, Fred, Anne, and Robert—have always been a source of strength for me.

Their successes have helped me understand the commitment needed to move to new levels. Their love is my greatest treasure.

To the people of Byron, Mexico, Roxbury, and Rumford, as well as Hanover, Andover, and Peru, I offer my heartfelt thanks for your support of learning and children in our community. This valley is a special place to teach and live.

And to all of my students, your daring and your scholarship have made Room 109 a place of celebration. Indeed, this book—like class—is ours, *together.*

1

Skidders, Chainsaws, and Sharing Stories

A Day in the Life of 109

My students have settled in. Andrea is huddled on the corner couch, knees up to her chin, devouring her third in a series of baby-sitter books. Off in the Writing Center, Matthew is at the computer synthesizing his research and interviews as a result of reading Frankl's *Man's Search for Meaning*. Eric is in the art room finishing up an oil painting that celebrates St. Exupery's *Wind, Sand, and Stars*, while Brooke, Amy, and Jarrod are out behind the school tending to the archaeological dig. At Meroby Elementary School, Allycia is working with an autistic boy, while just down the hall Janel edits a fourth-grader's short story. Back in class, Donna is catching up on her Spanish homework, and Dustin, eyes closed, is listening to his Walkman and will probably be fast asleep in a matter of minutes. Others of my student colleagues are composing songs, constructing models, and creating worlds.

It's a typical day.

It hasn't always been this way.

First Lesson

My first real "teachers" wore steel-toed boots and jeans and taught a seventh-period class in reality. They carried over-sized Igloo coolers, and most of them chewed tobacco. They loved trucks; and as a first-year high school English teacher, I figured their sole purpose in life was to make sure that I never became a second-year high school English teacher.

In the distance, one lone boy dressed in a sweat-stained T-shirt came clomping down the hall for seventh-period NOVA (Northern Oxford County Vocational Area) English. He carried the trademark cooler and seemed to be guided by his formidable boots. He looked harmless.

"How are you? I'm Mr. Kent."

"Hey. It's Brent."

He dropped his cooler, collapsed onto a chair at the back of the room, stripped off his T-shirt, and threw his heavy work boots on top of the desk, tilting his chair against the wall.

"What a fuckin' day."

I leaned over the lectern. My mind raced, and I quickly countered, "No shit."

Brent didn't flinch.

Again, my mind labored to make this work. "Listen," I said, as if we were hunting buddies. "If we use this kind of language, you're going to get kicked out of school, and I'm going to get fired."

"Yeah, you're right," he said wiping his face with his T-shirt, then tossing it to the floor.

A victory had never felt sweeter. And to think I had never taken an education course.

But the lesson was not over.

Each used the "f-word" habitually, as noun, verb, adjective, and in some contexts that created firsts for the English language. How did I handle it?

"Listen, we've got to watch our language." I sounded like Mr. Rogers. I felt naked, useless, absolutely lost. I'd worked with teenagers for thirteen years, and here I was stammering and stumbling about as if I'd never spoken with a kid before. Within five minutes of my junior/senior NOVA class, I knew I'd made the dumbest mistake of my professional life. I wanted to be back in the quiet corridors of the university with my first-floor office and leisurely lunches.

"Seriously, *guys*." That was it. I was dead. I knew it immediately. One simple word opened the door.

"Come on, *guys* . . ."

"Gee, *guys*," another mouthed.

The room exploded. I pushed the button on the intercom. "May I help you?" In contrast to 109, the secretary's voice was pleasant; I felt as though I should be ordering a flannel shirt from L. L. Bean.

"Help me? You sure can, Babe–be." A boy wearing a John Deere hat grabbed his crotch, and the room exploded.

"I need some help. Could you send down Mr. Blackman or Mr. Rowe?"

Mr. Rowe, the principal, arrived in a matter of seconds. With the wag of a finger and a couple of well-chosen words, "You, out," two boys strode out of my classroom, coolers and all.

The next three weeks proved to be the worst of my professional life; far worse than Army boot camp at Fort Knox and food poisoning while studying soccer in Sao Paulo, Brazil. During seventh period, I called for help over the intercom almost every other day. Fortunately, my administrators were always there for me.

The only sustained quiet in seventh period came when I passed out fourth-grade grammar sheets that I had discovered in the bottom of a file cabinet in my room.

CIRCLE THE CORRECT ANSWER:
I (was were) going to the store when I saw the accident.

These eighteen- and nineteen-year-old men caused little trouble while doing work sheets. They finished the exercises with varying degrees of success. We would do twenty examples in each class and then correct them. The correcting took half the time.

"How much off?" they'd ask. "How much off?" In the end it wasn't a matter of learning the correct usage; they cared about the score.

"What'd you get?"

"Forty-five."

"Goddamn. I got a fifty-five! Smoked you!"

I used these sheets as a dentist uses Novocain, and they took up thirty minutes of the forty-five-minute class period. The other fifteen minutes?

"I'll tell you one thing, Mister. Them Lucky Charms ain't sitting too good today," said Brent fanning the fetid air around his desk.

"John Deere? That skidder's the biggest piece of shit in the woods."

"Chevy's got no balls. Ford's for men."

"Steve, I heard you worked the heavy machinery down at the shop today. Wheel barrel's a bitch, ain't she?"

My college-bound classes were fine. In fact, within ten days I had already discovered how comfortable it was to turn aside the lectern, close up the desks into a circle, and sit right along side of them. The conversations challenged me. They were fun and interesting, and made me think in ways that my university students never had. In Room 109, I felt inspired. But then, seventh period.

I tried a little of everything with NOVA. One day I asked the guys about their "vehicles." The Ford and Chevy debate waged on until . . .

"What do you drive, Kent?" asked Brent.

Ah—ha! My sleek, jet black sports car. *This is it!* "A Mazda RX-7."

"Tin shit. How do you start her up, with a can opener?"

They asked me about fishing. I didn't like fishing but had enough smarts not to admit it. Next, they asked about hunting. This time I didn't think. "I don't believe in hunting." Butchered again.

As the days went on the NOVA boys discovered I wrote poetry. They were merciless. When my soccer players popped in to see "coach," there was more of the same.

"Pretty boys."

"Preppies."

Needless to say, once word spread among the team, none of my players ever came to see me again during last period.

Finally, one day at the end of September, about twenty-five work sheets into the quarter and four suspensions from school later, I learned the lesson.

It had been a long day. My soccer team returned from an away match at about ten P.M. the night before. My four college-bound classes demanded all of my attention. My study hall had exploded and sapped the rest of my energy. By seventh period, I couldn't have cared less.

The NOVA boys shuffled into class after their workday. I didn't re-place the lectern or rearrange the room into a horseshoe. I just sat in the circle, figuring I could take whatever they had to dish out for forty-five minutes. As always, Brent and a couple of other guys started dumping on the "tin knockers," those who opted to work in metal trades instead of wood harvesting. After the same old jabs, the con-versation turned.

"It'll cost forty-five bucks," argued Scott about Bob's speeding ticket.

"No way. Seventy-five in a fifty is going to be ninety bucks. For sure."

"Nope," I said casually. "Twenty-five over is sixty bucks for a first timer."

Most of them furrowed their brows and froze in place, as in that E. F. Hutton commercial. Except for giving the answers to work sheets, this was the first time I had said anything remotely interesting to them.

"How do you know?"

"Ha! Kent got busted for tearing ass in his little soup can."

"I didn't get busted (you frigging nitwit). I used to be a cop."

Their heads swung around, mouths agape. That was it. *A common ground*. Actually, I was on one side and they were on another, but in a way we both spoke the same language.

As a nineteen-year-old in college, I began working as a summer cop on the coast of Maine. My plans were to get a degree, work full time as a police officer, and go to law school at night. From my nearly three years as a policeman, I had a ton of war stories. Car accidents. Bar fights. Drugs raids. Dead bodies. With these, I had a captive audience.

We took up the whole class with stories. I told a few of mine; they told a few of theirs. The conversations ran the full spectrum.

"My old man's been in Thomaston for two years. He's supposed to get out in six months."

"Bobby tried to outrun the cops on his half-cylinder shitbox. Thing is, he forgot about one thing: gas–O–line."

They left laughing, smiling, and asking questions just as my college-bound kids did, though the questions weren't exactly the same.

"Was your cruiser a 405? I bet she kicked ass when you punched it."

"You really put your hand in his brains? What'd it smell like?"

"Did you use hollow points with your 357?"

"What did you really do with the pot?"

I took up my usual post in the doorway as they clomped out. One young man gave me a friendly slap on the shoulder without saying a word. A couple of others passed by, saying, "See ya tomorrow, Kent." And Brent? Well, he just smiled and shook his head.

Even now, I don't ever remember feeling so good at the end of a class. I was home.

That night, while celebrating with a pizza and back-to-back episodes of *M*A*S*H*, I thought a lot about NOVA. The very next day, I proposed moving our class from the last period of the day to seven-thirty in the morning, before school started and before the NOVA guys went off to work for five hours in the woods or shops. They agreed, even with the stipulation that they could not be late more than three days a quarter. For Bob, who lived just across the street from the school but was *not* a morning person, getting up forty-five minutes earlier was tantamount to memorizing an act from

Hamlet. The solution? On most mornings, the guys took turns stopping by Bob's house or phoning to roust him out of bed.

Once we moved our class to seven-thirty in the morning, I never called for help again, and I never kicked out another student. I wish I could say I didn't use work sheets, but I did. Every once in a while, I needed a total break, and I dragged a few sheets out. But mostly, we told stories and then wrote about them. We read sections from books, newspapers, or sporting magazines. We even wrote a number of complaint letters.

> I can't believe you let your workers go out for a couple of beers at lunch time. Them are newcleaer submarines their working on!!!! Just what we need some drunk touching off one of them things!!!! Smarten up!!!!!!!

The response from the shipbuilder's public relation's officer? "Only a small minority of our workers imbibe at lunchtime." That response made all of us feel a lot better.

In NOVA, I no longer talked about things outside the students' world. We began with skidders and chainsaws, cops and getting a good job. We ended with honest conversations on our missions in life (though we never used the word *mission*).

I brought in guests, like a friend who hired people down at the local paper mill. I had never seen these young men so well mannered and so savvy. That day, NOVA English could have been a morning seminar at Choate. As my friend Kenric Charles always says, "They know who butters their bread."

In time, these young men began to trust me, and I them. They admitted how embarrassing it had been at the beginning of the year to trudge up through the whole school for seventh-period English class in their sweaty vocational uniforms of T-shirts, jeans, and steel-toed boots.

"Clomp, clomp, clomp. Everybody stares," said Bob. "It's humiliating."

I also became sensitized to how the institution *and* I had treated students from this program. Everybody referred to them as the "NOVA boys."

When they left my classroom that June, in my eyes these young men were poets and scholars, writers and thinkers. They had read and watched *King Lear* and its Japanese counterpart *Ran*. Furthermore, all of them knew that "Mrs. Macbeth was a real bitch." Each left with a completed résumé and cover letter, as well as a guarantee that they could count on me for a reference. Perhaps most important of all, they knew that "pencil pushers" like Mr. Kent weren't half bad.

And what about the pencil pusher? Well, for one thing I drive a truck now, and I've learned my lesson. It is, perhaps, one of the most valuable I have learned.

All of my students—college bound or woods bound—see the world through eyes with a variety of limited experience. They have their own "world visions" and language, and I have mine. My role as teacher must be to recognize and validate where my students are as people and as learners. Sometimes "where they are" is difficult (painful?) to accept, as when students use racial slurs or foul language. But if I am honestly going to help them move toward that next level of understanding and awareness, I can't wish that they acted differently or knew more. They are who they are, and I must begin there, not where I wish they were.

"There is an assumption," says Yale child psychiatrist James Comer, "that learning is a kind of mechanical process—that you give information, kids take it in, they process it and give it back to you—or store it and remember it forever—and can act on it. That's not true. It is much more complicated. The reason we learn has a lot to do with our past experiences and our relationships with important others. We are motivated to learn out of relationships" (Young and Rubicam Foundation 1991, 77).

It's not news for most teaching practitioners that learning is complex and is certainly much more involved than passing out work sheets, assigning number grades, or writing a one- or two-word comment on an essay: "Awesome!" "Very good." And exactly what is an eighty-three?

Our students learn when a caring adult finds a way to connect. We all learn by sharing our stories.

Another Lesson

A few days after I received a state teaching award in a surprise school-wide assembly, a loud knock came at my classroom window. There, out on the lawn, smiling broadly, two years out of high school, stood Brent and his cousin Aaron, a fellow NOVA student.

"Kent!"

"Hey!"

"Saw you on the tube the other night, Big Guy. Good for you," said Brent.

"Thanks a lot. Crazy, huh?"

"Nah. We knew you could do it," he said peering over the window sill at my class full of students.

We traded a few pleasantries. Both boys eyed the girls in class and then were off. "Gotta be going. Just wanted to stop by to see *the man*."

As they strode off across the lawn to their pickup truck, I recalled a moment with Brent two years earlier.

It was my twenty-two-minute duty-free lunch break, shared for the past seven years with my colleague and friend Anne Wood. Brent appeared at my door and stood quietly, waiting to attract my attention. Some of the "smart" kids regularly barreled right in during my lunch. Not Brent. He knew what lunch break meant for working people.

"You got a minute?" he asked, once he had caught my eye.

"Sure." I stepped into the hallway, curious about Brent's quiet, understated demeanor.

"I was wondering if you could write me a recommendation?" he asked in a soft voice I had only heard once or twice before.

"Absolutely. When do you need it?"

He gave me the details and handed over the form from the technical college.

"I'll try to do it tonight or by Friday at the latest," I said.

"Thanks a lot. I appreciate it," he said. "Still got your winter car on the road?" he asked, catching me off guard.

"Yeah. I don't take out the Mazda until May."

"Well, bring her down to the shop."

I looked at him curiously.

"I'll change the oil in her."

It took me a moment to get it. "You don't have to do that," I said, embarrassed, almost speechless at his generosity.

"Hey, fair is fair," he replied.

Fair is fair.

Another lesson learned.

2

Room 109

Opening Day

On the first day of school, my new students settle in quietly. In classes with over twenty-six kids, I pull the coffin—Ryan's project in celebration of Edgar Allan Poe—into the circle of desks for extra seating. As rooms go at Mountain Valley, 109 is small.

For the past four years, almost every opening class has been uncomfortably quiet. Many students have heard about this class from their sisters, cousins, or friends. Others, like Amy, have only walked by.

> Last year as freshman I would walk by class and always want to go inside and see all the wonderful pictures and artwork. This year I got to do this. I can remember loving to go to English class at the end of a hard day and sit on a comfortable couch and not have bright florescent lights shinning in my face. The room kind of reminds me of my own room at my house.

Still others know the room from the previous year by the large signs hanging in the doorway at the end of each quarter:

It's portfolio day!
(Don't you just feel good all over?)

I find a seat and look slowly around the class. The students look so smart, are so good looking, and seem so ready to learn. I repeat a silent invocation: "Don't screw them up, Kent. Give them your best." Then I begin.

"Welcome to Room 109. I hope together we'll have an incredible year." They introduce themselves, and I pass out a letter similar to the following:

9

My Dear Students,

Welcome to Room 109. I want you to know that I'm happy to have you here. Together in English class this year we'll make music and write stories, tell jokes and read books. In short, we'll work, play, and learn. There are times when you won't much care for English, Room 109, or me. Things will get hard and hectic, and you'll be stressed out. Don't worry, that's normal. Sometimes learning is difficult; it's a struggle. Sometimes learning is like slow dancing and takes no effort at all. My advice? Let it happen . . . and *work, for the night is coming.*

Now, about my room. Stop reading this letter for a second and look around. I put stuff up on the walls because it makes me feel at home—it makes me feel comfortable. I hope it does the same for you. If you have something you'd like to put up, go for it.

Behind my desk are photographs of family and friends. Feel free to go over and take a look. You'll see pictures of my teams, too. Above the door is one of the State of Maine soccer teams I took to England. We had a blast. Just to the right of my desk is a poster of the first championship team in any sport at Mountain Valley High School: the 1989 MVC Soccer Champs. They were the best people. Also behind my desk are a collection of pictures of students who graduated over the past few years. Oh yeah, and the Red Sox T-shirt up on the curtain rod? That's Jamie Ippolito's. *We both love the Sox!*

Room 109 has history. This is the place where Craig Dickson put his hand through the window. The place where the lacrosse team held its first practice. Here, too, is where Janet Hoyle stood up one day and said, "I'd like to sing the class a song that I wrote." 109 is where *The Book of Cutt* was composed. Borrow it and have some laughs.

In this room I venture to guess that thousands of gallons of Mountain Dew and Diet 7-Up have been consumed at night and on weekends. It's also where Duncan MacIsaac gave me a special gift (*don't ask*), Jenn Nisbet conducted my funeral, and Mike Gawtry body slammed me because I was being a "royal jerk." It's where Amy Law announced, "Mr. Kent, I think you've lost your mind." To which Matt Irish responded, "Well, everyone knows that." And finally, in this very room Amy Welch and Dave Kasregis read ALOUD the letters of James Joyce—you'd have to read the letters to understand just how *incredible* that is!

English is a funny subject. As far as I'm concerned, English is everything. Some days we sing or build; others days we paint or hike. Every day we're reading, writing, and talking. You might get a bit concerned when you read the letters from former students in a moment. Don't worry, you'll do fine.

Now me. A warning: You will discover in time that I am not perfect. In fact, you may have already discovered that. (No comments!) Like you, I have good days and bad days. I work hard at trying to be fair and treating everyone well. I never succeed. *Never.* I always end up hurting someone somehow. I'm sorry for whatever stupid, insensitive, ignorant thing I might do to you. But please know that I'm trying the best I can. If you do the same, we'll have a whiz-banger of a year together.

Over the years in Room 109 we have studied a bit of everything, including English literature and quantum physics, poetry and infinity, commas and history, fiction and projectile vomiting, black holes and teaching, music, diversity, men, womyn, art, Tolstoy, Stevensian Thought, Frost, and drooling. We do everything and anything because English is just that: reading, writing, speaking, listening, performing, observing, cooking, and a whole lot more.

This year's theme in Room 109 is balance. We need balance to stand, to talk with others, and to laugh at ourselves. We need balance for poetry, novels, movies, sentences, and paragraphs. Balance plays a vital role in sports, in relationships, in classrooms, in families, in eating, and in swimming. Heck, without balance you wouldn't be able to sit where you're sitting or read what you're reading. So, it's important stuff.

This year you'll be writing your own book. It's called a portfolio. Look closely, for no matter what you've heard, *portfolio* is not a four-letter word. Really. Also, you need to know that most of the time in here you are in charge. That's weird, but you'll get used to it. Trust yourselves, for very soon you will be out in that big, wide, screamer of a world doing life on your own. Looking at it that way, English class ain't nothing.

My phone number is 364-2953. You may call me if you have a problem or if you just want to chat. Please don't call after nine in the evening. I'm old and I need my "handsome sleep." No wise comments. *Quiet! I can hear what you're thinking!*

So, that's it. Now I'll pass around letters from former students. Enjoy. Their ghosts are sitting beside you. Listen, ghosts or not, you should know they all survived.

Welcome. I'm glad you're here.

Your Loving English Teacher,
Richard Kent

P.S. For next class write a first draft, five-page, double-spaced, spell-checked, autobiographical sketch. This is a first draft freewrite, so don't worry about grammar stuff right now. Just write with reckless abandon! Also for next class you will need one *large* three-ring binder and a journal book. And finally (!), your class, 6/7 Blue, is responsible for reading and responding to portfolios at the end of second quarter in mid-January. Plan on spending either Saturday or Sunday morning here in school. Your *keeper* (parent or guardian) is invited to come in to read and respond, too! The more the merrier.

The letters that my former students write during their last week of school make my new students wonder, laugh, and shake their heads. In a very few cases each year, kids go to our Guidance Department and drop my course. Fair enough.

Dear Incoming Student,
   Welcome to Coach Kent's English class. I can honestly tell you that you have quite a year ahead of you. You will write more than you have ever written before, you will read more than you have ever read before, and as long as you keep your mind open, you will learn more than you ever have before. The class that you are taking is not just a class of literature, but more importantly, it is a class of Life. Good luck and enjoy.
                                             Sincerely,
                                             Kathy M.

Dear Incoming Student,
   Prepare yourself for a year-long journey through books and poetry, writing and music, laughter and drama.
   When you first hear of the workload in Room 109, you are probably going to want to drop this class then and there. Don't. Though the work seems almost impossible at first, you will soon discover that writing five papers in one quarter is not that big of a deal.
   It's a good idea to make yourself a calendar showing when you plan to have certain parts of your portfolio done. Let me assure you that staying up past midnight to write during the last couple of weeks is not fun.
   Your first draft of a paper is never going to be perfect, so try not to prevent yourself from writing because you feel that what you have to

say isn't good enough. Be concerned about finishing your first draft. What you've written can always be fixed up later.

If you have a study hall, take your paper to the Writing Center! There should be someone there who will be glad to edit.

Good luck. Try to be different and creative . . . there's nothing more boring than "traditional."

Sincerely,
Josie B.

Dear Student,

If you take English and get Mr. Kent, don't worry. It's the easiest class you'll ever have. He doesn't give any homework. You don't have to read any books. It's great! He let's you fool around as much as you want, and he's a real nice guy. If you haven't had a lot of work before, don't worry because you certainly won't here. If you are fortunate to get Kent's class, I will leave you with a 2-word thought . . .

JUST KIDDIN'!

Sincerely,
Brian T.

I believe these letters create a scaffolding, a bridge from student to student, past and present. At first the idea of instructional scaffolding came about as a way to effectively teach reading and writing (Langer and Applebee 1986). But this model can be used in other ways as well. In this case it is to learn more about a class and its teacher.

The best part about using letters from former students? They're real. They're honest. They connect.

After sharing the letters, I read a selection of poems written the previous year by 109ers. I practice my reading and work hard to present in my best voice. (I've included a few of these poems in the section "Full Contact Poetry.") I also read one of mine; usually a poem in celebration of summer or my students.

Then, I hand out model portfolios from the previous year. I've debated this practice on and off for a couple of years, worrying that the kids might be overwhelmed. Ultimately, after talking with many of my student colleagues, I decided to show the new students what's expected.

Most students page through these books of student work in dead silence. The majority can't believe the amount of work from a single nine-week quarter; each three-ring binder is stuffed. They look closely at the assessment sheets in the front where the final quarter grades appear. I direct them to the cover sheets, a portfolio's table of contents. They read with interest the personal letters written in response to each completed portfolio—there's one by me, a couple by students, and one by another adult, usually a parent or guardian. Then, I point out the section that includes each of the papers and their rough drafts.

Inevitably, someone whispers to a neighbor, "I can't do all this."

It's then that I step in. "This is a lot of real work; but don't worry, you can do it. Last year, 117 different kids did." Often, they don't look convinced.

Next, to lighten the mood, I give a twelve-minute slide show of fun moments from the previous year. I play some of my favorite music to accompany the 140 photographs. The show begins with Kermit the Frog singing "Rainbow Connection," moves on to "Friends in Low Places" by Garth Brooks, and ends with Louis Armstrong singing "What a Wonderful World."

Our discussion about the slide show focuses on storytelling with and without words. I ask what the Native Americans might mean by "we truly learn by the sharing of stories."

With that, our year—and our story—begins.

Responding to Autobiographies

Since we now have block scheduling with ninety-minute periods every other day, my students have two evenings and an entire school day in which to write their life's story. (They think I'm generous, too.)

I make it clear that their piece does not have to be revised. "Just do the best you can with the paragraphing and punctuation and all. I want to hear about your lives. The English stuff can wait." I ask for first draft work for a couple of reasons.

Michael Armstrong's (1992) discussions at the Bread Loaf School of English about revision have stayed with me. "I'm a bit nervous about revision," he admitted. "It sort of homogenizes work." Indeed, there's something exciting about reading first drafts and hearing the unfettered writing voices of my new students. Getting the raw, off-the-cuff, here-I-am-like-it-or-not kind of writing helps me come to know them.

First-draft writing comes from the gut. It's ingenuous and straightforward. My students don't have a chance to "doctor" up their thinking or their writing. In truth, *they are who they are or who they would like to be* in a first draft. Additionally, reading a first draft helps me pick up on basic problems in composition and technique. If a student automatically paragraphs fairly well or has a rich variety of sentence construction, I plan my instruction accordingly. I relish first drafts for the creativity and the honesty.

For most kids, especially marginal writers (or should I say nonwriters?) who have had little success, this first assignment is a tough one.

"Mr. Kent. Mr. Kent! I ain't never written five pages on anything in my whole life," announced Richard, a boy who had failed ninth-grade English with a fifty-two the previous year.

"Well, give it your best shot," I said. "I know you can do it."

"But what am I going to write about me?"

"Anything. Everything. Whatever you'd like."

"I don't have nothing to write about."

"Okay. Let's come up with some ideas."

As a class we finished the statement "I am the one who . . ." and came up with a list of twenty-five topics including family and favorite malls, future occupations and books we've tried to read and hated. Since the assignment is a first-draft freewrite, I tell the students they should write as much as they can about topics they're interested in and then move on. I emphasize yet again that this is a rough draft.

Five *whole* pages after a long illiterate summer is a shocker, but the students need to know what they are getting themselves into. (This is one reason I am all for readjusting our school calendar to be in sync with learning needs, not turn-of-the-century farming demands.)

Here is Richard's autobiography, the longest "thing" he has ever written in his life:

> My name is Richard. I live in Peru (Maine). I live with my mother and stepfather and my brother. My mother and father got divorced when I was two. I think it was probably the best from what I've heard. On my father's side there is three kids and there mother and my dad. The cool thing about it is that I can live anywhere I want. I was raised in Rumford but then at age ten we moved to Peru. That was probably the turning point in my life. I think it was better for me to move to Peru because now I come up to this school and see my old friends and say I am glad that didn't happen to me. When I was just little I was an innocent kid believe it or not. But then as I grew up I hit that got to fit in stage. I use to be a little rebel. I always was

hanging around the wrong crowd for some reason. No matter what it always was the wrong one. For instants this summer I got accused for a bunch of stuff down the pond just because who I hang around with the wrong crowed. I don't really have a best friend I just have a bunch of friends and a few are in this class. Peter, Joe and Mike they are a little weird some times but you learn to like them. I knew Peter since third grade and that is when we started playing football and baseball together. I play a variety of different sports. Like lacrosse is my favorite but I have not much experience. Yet I play it any ways. If I could change anything about myself it would be not to be as lazy and realize how much school means to me. If I could change anything about my friends it would be that they all could be smart and able to like almost everyone that they see instead of cutting them all down. I would like to be in a different country right now because of this paper but you might have to do even more there. And I would not like to go to Alaska. I like to snowmobile but not that much. I have achieved a lot of little things but not really any big ones yet. When I was in 5–7 grade I made the honor roll every quarter. I think it was because I never had barely any home work and I was in a smaller school so you were more recognized. The best thing about school is your class actually. Because you seem to listen what everyone has to say and you give them a chance. I am not saying this to get a good grade either. The worst thing about school is how some of the teachers just drag the day on and on. With the same boring old work sheets and the same old text books day after day. That is why I think portfolios sound good. I have been challenged through the years but this one sounds good and hard. The music I like to listen to is pearl jam and old rock and roll like neil young and I have to mix it up with a little bit of country even. I have a bunch of different hobbies, I like to hike water ski snowmobile and to play lacrosse and hopefully next year I can play soccer again. When I grow up I would like to have a wife and no kids. Because if money ever got tight I wouldn't want my get to made and have no friends. Because if I had a kid I would like him to be intelligent and the best at every thing or at least try his hardest. Speaking of jobs I would like to go in the air force like my cousin Robert. And if I liked I would stay in there the twenty years an collect money after and get a little odd job to keep me from rotten. I don't like when you see a little kid on the street smoking or doing drugs. Every one wines and cries about getting cancer because of the mill but I hope that don't think smoking is going to help. The best cousin I have is either Robert or my cousin Chris. I can tell is going to have a bad life because he is a little mouth piece and he will do any thing once. I try as hard as I can to help him but I shouldn't talk. I have never tried drugs and I have tried smoking once. I thought I was going to die so I never tried that again. I guess it was one of those peer pressure things. the cool thing about my life is that I am pretty active and athletic. But then again I don't play that many sports. I am not the kind of person who needs to get his way. Just ask my friends they will tell you that. The best time I had in my life was probably when I was a little kid and we went to South Caroline. The scariest part of my life was at either tumble down in Peru, or the Tumbledown in Weld. The one in Peru because just last week I climbed the tree line with sandals on it gets pretty slippery and pretty scary but I did it any way. And at the weld one I was climbing the chimney and my pack got caught on a tree and I almost went for a loop. The things I have found out in life are never give up no matter how late. If you do what you always do you might not be very interesting. I don't like to get involved in fights but when there is Jack Peters around your scared of getting beat on. I don't hang around with the type that like to fight. Because then you always end up getting in to them. I don't like to hang around the cocky type because they always us you. And the part I hate most about school is they don't make it fun. Who wants to sit in the same room with the same text book all year round. Last year there was teacher that said I get paid every year no matter what I make you do. The thing about teachers in this school is that they don't care about you. But the feelings that the teacher will get from me is that you treat me bad and I will treat you bad. Well that is pretty much my whole life and what I like and don't like.

Richard

I respond to each student's autobiographical sketch with a personal letter. Richard's piece excited me. It was so much more than I had hoped for. Having known his ninth-grade English scores, I was fearful that I would receive little or nothing. Not so. I love to be amazed by my students in this way. Here is my note in return:

Dear Richard,
    This is a brilliant autobiography! Expressive, honest, intelligent. You really know yourself and your life, don't you? Incredible. Even though you've had a few downs in your life, you don't let them get to you. It's cool how you look at things. I admire that. You said you got honor roll back in 5th grade through 7th grade. You can do that

here, too. *Really!* REALLY! The Air Force could be a good choice for you. But since you're only in the 10th grade, you have plenty of time to think. Oh . . . I can just see you getting stuck in Tumbledown's Chimney Trail with your pack. HA! I know where you got wedged in . . . it's a tight spot, isn't it? It's a great view on top. I love the lake up there, too. Well, enough. Congratulations! You're passing 10th grade English. If I were you, I'd use this autobiography for a formal paper. Get an editor in the Writing Center to edit it for you and you're on your way. Good luck, Richard. I'm glad you're here!

YLET,
Rich Kent

Students like Richard who have had little success in school are amazed when they receive a serious written response to their work from the teacher. It seems pretty clear to me now, if I take them seriously by writing this letter (and others) they'll take English and me more seriously as well. Does this transformation happen immediately? Not usually, especially for students who feel out of place in school. Sometimes it takes months for these young people to trust me and to understand that I truly care about what they have to say and how they say it.

During the first week of school, I set up Richard with Sarah, one of the Writing Center editors who is extraordinarily kind and unusually gifted at working with students who labor. The Writing Center is housed in our media center. Students may leave a class or a study hall with permission from their academic teacher to work in the Center with a peer writing tutor, a student from Room 109.

Sarah began working with Richard during workshop time in class. I asked her to help him revise his autobiography and make it a "formal paper" in his first-quarter portfolio. Unfortunately, in that first week Richard lost the computer disk with his life story, and he had not kept a backup disk. Sarah, being the kind soul that she is, helped him type the whole paper over again—that was the last time he lost his disk that year.

Richard did not receive an honors grade on his portfolio assessment, but he kept his head above water. He also knew he had two people on his side who cared.

Using autobiographies for comparative analyses

For first-year 109ers, autobiographies provide a place to return throughout the year. These essays are ideal sources to scout for paper and journal ideas. For those who join English 109 for a second year, many write comparative analyses of their two autobiographies. Because these papers are personal and authentic, the level of introspection is usually quite sophisticated and offers my young colleagues a unique look at their emerging selves.

"I am not who I was a year ago," writes Sandra. "I have made decisions in the past twelve months that have changed my life and who I thought I was."

Creating a Dialogue Through Letters

In response to my letters about their life stories, each student writes a letter to me. This exchange is vital at the beginning of the year because it is real and it helps us build our relationship.

Here is my letter in response to Lindy's autobiography. A senior student, Lindy is spending her second year in my class.

> Dear Lindy,
>
> I was so impressed with your letters this summer. I wish I would have had the time to write personally more than once in response. You left an impression on me that is lasting.
>
> Your writing voice has grown in wonderful ways. There's a confidence that shines and an ability—a talent?—you show of being able to "see" all sides of things. Yes, at moments you sound a bit young or uninitiated, but at other times you sound worldly and interested, confident and interesting.
>
> I know what a passionate friend you are. You are mentioned in many journals and papers not to mention letters. You are a good friend. I liked reading what I did about you by your friends; it gives me hope. Many people will be blessed by having you in their lives.
>
> It's fun to read about you and Frost Motor. I can see all the garage guys coming in and chit chatting with you. This is a story in the making, don't you think? It's not usual that a young woman would be in this world. The story of this—it could be fictionalized—could be interesting and fun. Think about the possibility.
>
> I would love to see you take chances with your reading this year. You have a great deal to learn from books . . . all of us do. Let's challenge you; let's see if we can move you to another level as a reader.
>
> I'm glad you're back here. I hope together we'll have a wonderful year. Best wishes, Lindy.
>
>   ylet,
>   Rich Kent

PS Your position in soccer is not all that important, is it? Being on the team with your friends and having good times is what it's about. I know you know this.

Dear Mr. Kent,

Thank you for such a positive response to my autobiography. It really made me feel better as a student in the Writing Center. Your letter has made me begin to feel more comfortable with myself and my thoughts in this class.

I'm glad that you were able to enjoy my letters this summer. I enjoyed writing them as well. I love to write letters to people. I swear I have written a letter every night since my friends have left for college.

I still do not see how my writing voice is changing or developing. I write the same as I always have, well, apparently not, but *I* still see it that way. It has always meant a lot to me that one sees all sides of something. I guess you kind of miss out if you do not consider all of the aspects. It's our own fault if we miss something good.

When you say that many people will be blessed by having me in their lives, I wonder, "Will they really, or does it just seem that way?" It's strange to think deeply about it because it just makes you dig deeper about yourself and you can really see yourself. I always try to be a great person to everyone. Everyone deserves respect and I try to give it all away. At the end of the summer towards the beginning of school, I got into this respect kick. If anyone disrespects me, I don't want to talk to them. It is a waste of time to bother. Yeah, I'm still the same old nice person, but my ways won't be as sincere.

Working at Frost Motor with my father was cool. All the guys were so funny. They always called me cutie and really made me laugh. I wish everyone could have the experience that I had. How come I never saw you there, Kent? Well, at least now you know the best place to go for car stuff is OBVIOUSLY Frost! Not only am I the cutest delivery girl around, I promote business, too.

Taking chances with my reading is very scary. I have never been a strong reader. If I'm not reading something that completely takes my attention away, I find it harder to enjoy and get through without quitting. Right now I am reading three books at the same time for English and psychology. Ahh. No problem though because so far I'm having luck with my choices. I am enjoying all three so right now things are A-OKAY with me. After I get these done, I'm up for a challenge. Most definitely a great revelation. We'll talk.

I'm glad to be back here, Mr. Kent and I am looking forward to an exciting and educational year in the Writing Center class. Don't forget, I'm up for anything.

Sincerely,
Lindy B.

PS I do know that my position as goalkeeper IS important, but I'd rather be having fun doing it than hating it. Oh well, I'm getting back into loving it. I've decided that there is no need to get myself worked up over something so petty. I am only being selfish anyway.

Writing to Build a Classroom Community

One of the ways I help build a community within the classroom and assist students in connecting with one another is by sharing parts of their writing in a synthesis. Once I have read and responded to all of the autobiographical pieces over the first weekend of school, I go back through each one and look for an interesting line or two. Then, I type them up.

To be sure, the reading of autobiographies, the writing of letters, and the development of a synthesis make for an incredibly long weekend. This year, I hunkered down behind my computer for most of the long Labor Day weekend. Still and all, these letters set the tone for the rest of the year. There's no substitute for communicating personally.

Here's a portion of what was an eleven-page synthesis. I make sure each student has a line in the collection.

> *Walk around feeling like a leaf.*
> *Know you could tumble any second.*
> *Then decide what to do with your time.*

Naomi Shihad Nye

My Dear Students,

As we have discussed, the Native Americans tell us that we truly learn by the sharing of stories. This weekend, after reading hundreds of pages of your life stories and responding to each of you in writing with my own thoughts, I feel I have learned a great deal. Most of all, I leave these stories with a feeling of satisfaction.

I loved the energy in your writing. Collectively, this is a powerful series of autobiographies. Your voices are clear and impassioned. Clearly, you live interesting lives. Most of you named the names of those you care for, offered detail upon detail, and shared the great and not-so-great moments of your lives. The way you wrote about friends and family amazed me. You talked maturely about relationships and influences. I admired your honesty and sensitivity. Are you sure you're teen-agers?

It is only right that I share some of the lines that helped shape my understanding of who you are. Listen closely and you will come to know . . .

The People of Room 109

I am the youngest of nine children, four sisters and four brothers.

I was brought up in an alcoholic family.

I have always had this dream to live on the Maine coast.

I fell down the stairs and went into a coma.

Woodcutting is a hobby I picked up from a teacher at Saint A. Saint John.

My father and my mother are in New York working construction.

After crashing several hundred times on my bike I realized the training wheels weren't training me for anything but a chair in the hospital.

I'm not sure I know what I want to do with my life. I find that my interests change frequently and I worry that I will never be able to be content with one career.

As a toddler, I spent my days at home because of my shyness.

A silly fantasy . . . You know how models get their pictures taken? Well, I would like to be in a magazine some day.

My father has been a very strong influence in my life.

My hundred mile hike was incredible and I'm glad I made time for it.

If I had to spend a day doing anything with anyone, I would go fishing with my grandfather . . . I was only four when my grandfather died.

I am a junior. I should be a senior, but like I said, "I've learned the hard way."

It put a lot of stress on my mother when I moved out.

Reading is my life.

My parents and I don't agree on anything.

I think the world has become a very hard place to live in.

The second friend I had was not even human, it was my neighbor's dog.

A lot of people feel sad/mad because I am a mother so young.

I've never met my biological father.

By the way, my mother cried when she read this autobiography.

I would like to become a neurologist.

It's important to be a good person.

And so a glimpse into the lives of the people of Room 109. Truthfully, some of your stories gave me hope for our school, our town, and our planet. Some of your life stories made me wince. Others made me cheer. If time permitted, I wanted to call you up on the phone and say, "Hey, how about we go out for a pizza and talk." But there's *rarely* enough time for stuff like that these days, is there?

I liked what you believed in: family, friends, pets, laughter, school, art, music, sentiment, passion, work, honesty, travel, nature, dance, celebrations, study, science, sports, singing, listening, talking, the mind, the heart, love, joy, silence, experience, the future, the past, the moments of the now, philosophy, pizza, reading, writing, questioning, arguing, film, the full moon, kissing, a deep fly ball, a good cry, black holes, quiet mornings, loud parties, meditating, details, colors, hugs, poetry, memories, wishes, the color purple, winter days, summer beaches, dreams . . . and life's moments of wonder.

This year, *together*, sharing our stories, we will come to know a bit more about being human. I look forward to all of our moments here in Room 109.

Always, Your Loving English Teacher,
Richard Kent

3

Learning to Learn with Portfolios

My portfolio is really a book that is all about me and my life.
Josh, a senior

At the end of each quarter, my students begin to sense what they are capable of producing.

> *To My Loving English Teacher . . . I wrote five one-thousand word papers, forty-eight one-page journal entries, read five books and did five projects this quarter. I even taught at the elementary school once a week. I've never worked so hard and done so much in my life . . . Why am I so happy?*
>
> Kate, a senior

At the end of each school year, they stack their four portfolios on top of one another, take a good hard look, and then write.

> *When I used to hear the word "portfolio" I never thought of it as a personal thing. I always thought of it as a bunch of required stuff put together in a binder. But this year I've learned the difference. My English portfolios are very special to me. My portfolio resembles me because everything written in my portfolio came from my mind and heart. I did it all myself. I look back on my portfolios now and I can't help but smile.*
>
> Jill, a sophomore

As with an artist's portfolio or sketchbook, the English student's portfolio is a representation of the student, her work, and her thinking, or "all about me and my life." The personal nature of these books creates a powerful sense of authorship and pride. A few years ago in her second-quarter reflection, Amy wrote:

> *So, you want to know about portfolios? It's the toughest test I've ever had in school. The funny thing is: I made it up and I had all the answers.*

24

During the last week of school in June, while working on their final reflections, many of my students lug these four books around with them as a kind of red badge of courage. These four binders represent hard work, accomplishment, and scholarship. In the end, the kids are proud of themselves, and they want to show their friends what they have created.

Why am I so happy? It's pretty simple, really. The students have accomplished real work and produced something of value.

The portfolio takes over your life. You are no longer a teen-age kid.
You become the "Journal-writing, paper-editing, book-reading, project-making,
no sleeping, super portfolio man.

Anthony, a junior

The Teacher at Portfolio School

We all learn by experience but some of us
have to go to summer school.
Peter De Vries

I didn't have a clue about portfolios until I did my own at The Bread Loaf School of English in Dixie Goswami and James Britton's "Coming to Know Your Classroom: Stories and Theories." I remember walking out of class the first day and asking a classmate, "I'm glad there aren't any tests in here, but exactly what do we have to do?" She looked at me with the same wide and panicked eyes that I am sure I had: "You got me."

The assignment, we discovered, was to develop a portfolio—a collection—focused on the theme of the class. Yet, amazingly, there were no amounts or specific requirements, save a few "suggested" books in the course description and handouts. Many of us relentlessly pursued Dixie and the class assistant, Betty Bailey, begging to be *told* what to do. Fortunately, they never gave in.

I had never felt so lost in my academic life as I did that first week or so at Bread Loaf. Finally, one day, I remember being curious about a book someone raved over during class. The next thing I knew I was huddled in the bowels of the Middlebury College library. There, I read and jotted down notes, all the while thinking, "No one assigned this. Why am I doing this?" At that moment, an epiphany of sorts, my learning and teaching life changed forever. I have never looked back.

All my academic life, except for a few isolated moments, I had been told what to write, what to read, and in a very real sense, what to think and feel. But that summer in the Green Mountains of Vermont, some very fine teachers trusted me to find my own way. I learned about my reading and writing, my thinking, my learning, and my teaching. That next fall when I returned to Room 109, I pulled the plug on the old Mr. Kent, and portfolios were born.

Bread Loaf made the difference for me. Creating my own portfolio helped me understand from the student author's point of view the organization, the anxiety, the flexibility, and all the rest that goes into creating one's own "language arts book." Yet, even without that summer experience, I would have continued to personalize my classroom by individualizing student work and my expectation of that work. In other words, I would have created a learner-centered classroom with or without portfolios.

As a writer myself, I recognized early on in my teaching career that writers need to be treated individually. After my Bread Loaf experience, I began to understand that readers and artists and thinkers— all learners—need to be treated individually, too. I just didn't realize that portfolios were one means to that end.

Friends of mine who have begun portfolios have tested them out with one class for half a year. Others tried them for nine weeks with all their classes. Still others, like me, have jumped right in. However teachers make this move toward a learner-centered classroom, it is a bold and frightening leap right into the lives of young learners.

Making the Leap to Portfolios

"No tests, no quizzes, and only one grade" for a thing called a portfolio. Just thinking about that late August announcement seven years ago makes my stomach do cartwheels. My students' faces lit up as if they'd heard a "no school" bulletin broadcast over the radio. The automatic applause gave way to a series of Yeses! with low arm thrusts, hoots, and high fives all around.

Once the noise quieted, I overheard one dread-locked skater whisper to a compatriot, "No tests? Party on, Dude!"

I plowed on, explaining that they would have free choice of books; however, I thought we would read a couple of books together later on in the year. (Depending on the class, we would read and act out *Hamlet* or *Macbeth*.) I could see the avid readers and the Stephen King fans salivating at the idea of free choice of books. But sadly, many of the students couldn't have cared less for this newfound freedom. Most weren't readers. They rarely read what was assigned, so this new scheme by Kent made absolutely no difference to them. Others, I discovered later on by reading their reflections, simply wanted to be told what to do, similar to my initial reaction at Bread Loaf.

> *Why do you make us think so much? Why can't you just give us a test?*
> Julie, a junior

Thinking back, more than eliminating tests and quizzes, opening up free choice of books took an incredible amount of chutzpa on my part. After all, up until then almost everything we did in 109 English revolved around books we read together and that I taught.

Although my classes before portfolios were fun and engaging, mine had been a fairly traditional approach, though, I suppose, some might disagree. Essentially, 109 was teacher centered: I chose the books, designed the tests, assigned the papers, led the discussions, and suggested projects. Indeed, I was in charge.

For the most part, I treated my twenty-five students as one. I moved them along as if they all had the same reading levels, the same interests, the same work schedules, the same home lives, and the same goal of heading off to a four-year college. (We were still homogeneously grouped at that time.) In learning terms my methods and assessments fit a few of my students well; however, I ignored, quite innocently, many of my young colleagues' learning styles and intelligences (Gardner 1983; 1993a). I offer no apologies because, except for my Bread Loaf experience, teacher-centered classrooms were pretty much all I'd ever known as both student and teacher.

> *Life is not a paragraph.*
> Graffiti on a building
> at Oxford University

It's clear. Focusing on one intelligence in a classroom is like living with only one of the five senses. Nurturing a variety of intelligences creates difference in a classroom, and difference creates wonder.

Certainly, before developing a portfolio pedagogy, I appreciated my students as individuals, but I did not allow for or nurture their individual intelligences with the kind of confidence and understanding that I do now. Reading Howard Gardner's theory of multiple intelligences helped me envision a classroom filled with the products of diverse learners. Now I understand the significance of representing ideas and texts with an oil painting, a song, a well-crafted cabinet, or an essay.

Connecting: Turning Theory into Practice

Before using portfolios and looking critically at my practice from a learner's point of view—an act I now call teacher research—my thoughts about the theory and philosophy of education paralleled Alex's thinking on *Walden*. "Mr. Kent," he wrote in a quarter-end reflection, "this book is pointless. It's all about life."

After studying at Bread Loaf and taking the leap to a workshop class with a portfolio pedagogy, my previous readings, studies, and thinking began to connect and make meaning. Truly, I was taken over by the idea of turning theory into practice. Indeed, thanks to my summer studies, I had become a learner again. Only now, my learning focused on my teaching.

Frank Smith's *Essays into Literacy*, Aidan Chamber's *Booktalk*, and Louise Rosenblatt's *The Reader, the Text, and the Poem*, books I had read before Bread Loaf, began to sizzle and demand another reading. Ted Sizer's *Horace's Compromise* and Jonathan Kozol's *The Night Is Dark and I Am Far from Home* started to find their way into this evolving plan, my vision for a learner-centered classroom.

A good example of this "connecting" is Bill Nave's talk at a Mountain Valley High School in-service just before I left for summer school. Bill taught at an alternative education school just down the road in Turner, Maine. A finalist for National Teacher of the Year, he spoke passionately about individualizing our practices. He urged us to be responsive to individual learners, saying, "People learn at different rates and in different ways." A warmth came over me as Bill spoke. I understood what he was saying, yet I did not have the experience in a public school setting to put his thinking into practice.

Here's part of a handout Bill offered:

The Paradigm Shift

Old Educational Ideas (the old paradigm)	New Educational Ideas (the new paradigm)
One size fits all	Look at individual needs/goals
Teacher as expert, a fountain of knowledge	Teacher as mentor, facilitator
Students as passive recipients	Students are active learners

Six-hour school day	School open from 7 A.M.–10 P.M.
Nine-month school year	Year-round school
Lock-step age-graded schooling	Multi-age continuous progress schooling
Textbook/curriculum driven	Student interest driven
Goal: acquiring facts and knowledge	Goal: learning how to learn, process, think, solve, apply, analyze, synthesize
One right and best teaching method	Many best methods, according to student needs
Students working individually, competitive	Students working cooperatively and collaboratively, teamwork
Schooling K–12 only	Schools as centers for life-long learning: open adult ed offerings for K–12 students; open K–12 classes for adult learners; combine resources of school and town library

At Bread Loaf, creating a portfolio, taking part in a workshop class, and discussing practice continually with my roommate, Tom DeCarlo of Vermont's Burke Mountain Academy, provided the insight and the modeling to help me change. Upon my return, not only could I grasp Bill's words and those of other master teachers, I knew I could do something with them.

The Stuff of Portfolios: Basic Requirements/109 Portfolio

> *Maybe I am a idiot, but at least I ain't stupid.*
> Forrest Gump

Imagine the chaos:
"Okay, boys and girls. In nine weeks I'd like you to pass in a portfolio. Do whatever you'd like."

During my second summer at Bread Loaf, this time at Lincoln College, Oxford University, my mentor Michael Armstrong delighted in calling me a "radical teacher." Maybe so, but *I ain't stupid.*

Unlike my portfolio experience at Bread Loaf where the final product was left entirely up to me, I decided to set some basic requirements for my Mountain Valley students. I knew I'd be setting many of them up for failure or at least a miserable experience without supplying some sort of expectation.

Here's what I ask my students to produce for one quarter, approximately nine weeks:

- three formal papers (a variety of genre encouraged), *highly drafted*, 600–1000 words, all drafts attached

- two informal papers, edited once, 600–1000 words, draft attached

- forty-eight, one-page journal entries of approximately 150 words each

- five books read

- handouts and notes taken

- three to five art projects and/or presentations over books or themes

- the reflection of the previous quarter

- *keeper* letter (parent, guardian, or significant adult letter response to the student's portfolio)

This is the stuff of an average portfolio in 109. "Average" is a relative thing when living and learning in a portfolio workshop classroom. Because of the highly individualized approach, portfolios take on lives of their own. They are acted upon by a multitude of forces, from classroom themes to school curricula, from individual student interests to current research in the teaching of English. The strongest force? Kari, Mike, Kathy, and all the other learners of Room 109.

Exactly what do I mean when I say that my students are "the strongest force" in developing a portfolio? Here's one small example. Let's say, after reading Kari's autobiography and chatting with her about books, I discover she's not a reader. Is five books in nine weeks a realistic goal for someone who can't remember the last time she read an entire book? No way. So, my focus with Kari is to set realistic reading goals through honest, straightforward talk. In some cases marginal students read two books per quarter; in other cases students might read eight. I don't announce to the entire class, "Hey, if you can't read five books, don't worry." Conversations are personal and ongoing with the ultimate goal of moving each student to his or her next level.

Transitioning to a portfolio pedagogy demanded a sharing that, at times, could be unnerving. For me, living with portfolios means giving over authority; for my students it is an acceptance of responsibility. New and exciting territory for both.

These basic requirements fit into our plans today but could change tomorrow or next week. Developing a portfolio pedagogy is a process, like writing a poem. You can't begin at the end with a final copy—in fact, in the portfolio classroom there is never a final copy. Anyone moving toward a portfolio pedagogy will create many drafts of his or her classroom practice by listening closely to student colleagues, by discussing practice with staff colleagues, by reading about practice from good books, and, perhaps, by going back to school. Begin with what you have, with what you know, and then shape it, like clay, into a classroom that reflects you and your students. Two things are vital when considering the shift to a portfolio pedagogy: (1) Students and teachers drive the curriculum, (2) Pedagogy is personal.

Our basic portfolio with five papers, five books, and so forth, serves as a guideline, a gauge, and sometimes a goal. Why these particular requirements? For one thing, there's a good deal of reading, writing, and the stuff of language arts for a nine-week quarter. This is a "tough test," but soon students discover that they provide both questions and answers.

Formal and Informal Papers

Formal and informal papers run the full range of genre as decided by the student. My only request is that the students seek diversity.

Students compose essays, personal narratives, fictional narratives, interviews, parodies, research reports, memoirs, newspaper articles, credos, obituaries, video narrations, biographies, comic strips, speeches, plays, poems, autobiographies, letters, and editorials. Often, they return to certain genres of writing they experienced in middle school or before. They also dream up their own *unique* genres as well.

Infinity

holds a logic of its own   Infinity has the ability to defy what we
define as "logic"   A good example of this would be in mathematics
1+1 equals 2, by our humanistic thinking   However, when dealing
with infinity, 1 and 1 make 1   one number and one number make
one number   There are three separate numbers, and yet, there is

one number in total   This "math" is reminiscent of Christianity's
Holy Trinity, where God the father, Jesus his son, and the holy spirit
are all one   Three are one and one is three   The whole is not
   only the sum of its parts, but is its parts   When the answers of
the two mathematical methods are compared, we find that they are
   different   Each sum does not equal the other   1 is not 2, by
   rational standards   This is where the full force of the paradox
takes effect   Each philosophy of math has a common goal—the
yearning for an answer   Each attempts to formulate the answer,
   and when the two answers differ, they impede each other's
   progress   We are trapped at the junction where one equals two,
which we feel cannot be   Consequently, we attempt to search for
a mediator in the realm of thought, and cannot find it   We are
            left with the question   that we began our
                  journey with   The question of
                        Infinity

David created a paper on "infinity" after our classroom discussions
and readings. His piece included a series of paragraph-like thoughts
strung together in a six-page paper attached with two rings. Physi-
cally, the paper has no beginning or ending; similarly, since we can
think about his thinking and about our own thinking *forever*, there is
no ending.

I encourage this kind of playful thinking and writing. In truth, this
is experimentation, and it helps my students uncover meaning. A
prime example of writing to learn.

4

Managing an English/ Language Arts Workshop

The Day-to-Day of a Portfolio Master

I'm fond of saying, "English is everything." For those just passing by and glancing in, sometimes Room 109 looks hectic. But in the midst of this beehive of activity, I am always there chatting and organizing, questioning and answering.

Come in to Period 3/4 Silver for a few minutes and follow me around. This class is heterogeneously grouped with twenty-three sophomores, juniors, and seniors. The class lasts ninety minutes and meets every other day.

10:00 A.M.

"Any projects to present today?"

A few kids chuckle.

"One project every two weeks," I remind them for the billionth time. "Spread them out. Please let's not have twenty-three presentations next Friday."

More laughter. Over half will be on Friday; however, that will change as the year progresses and as all of us get more organized.

"Would you like a journal entry today?" I ask.

"I don't have time," says Rachel, matter-of-factly. "I've got to get to a computer because Shelly said she'd edit my next draft during last period."

"Okay, Rachel, hold on for a minute."

Rachel's not pleased. She wants to leave. She really has work to do and because she doesn't have a home computer, school computer time is precious.

"Does anyone want a journal entry?"

"I gotta work, too," says Wayne. "Sarah's waiting in the Writing Center to help me with this stupid credo."

"A credo's about *you*, isn't it?" cracks Brian.

"Ha. Ha. Ha," says Wayne.

"Okay," I say. "I guess that's it for the day. Don't forget we're beginning our discussion on relationships next class. Come get a pass if you're heading to the computer lab or Writing Center."

I begin the task of scribbling a list of names for those going to the Writing Center. The kids call out their names.

"Brian."

"Wendy, Vic, and Darcy."

"Who's going to 213?" (the computer room).

More names.

Once they've left, twelve kids remain in Room 109. Samantha and August trade papers for an edit. Peter lies back on the couch pretending to read. Kimberly is a journal freak—she's got her head down, writing furiously. Two other students, seniors on independent studies, are not here. They're at the elementary schools working on writing with younger students.

"I've got to go to the art room to see Ms. Wing," says Barb, returning my personal copy of Lois Lowry's *The Giver*. "I need to schedule a time to start my airbrush project over this," she says pointing toward Lois Lowry's book.

"Is this a good time for her?" I ask, not wanting to dump a student on my friend, Chris Wing.

"No problem. She told me to stop by. It'll only take a minute."

I write the pass. Barb leaves.

"Mr. Kent," says Joey, "I need another book."

Joey's not a strong reader. My eye catches *The Giver*. "You haven't read this one, have you?"

He hasn't.

"This is an awesome book about a boy in the future. You'll love it. I read it in an afternoon."

Joey cocks his head as if to say, "This is Joey, Mr. Kent. I don't do reading, remember?" But, when he sees it's not a huge book, he buys in and heads back to his seat.

"Can we listen to some of your music?" asks Andrea.

Sally groans.

"Anybody mind? Other than Sally, of course," I joke. Kids laugh. Sally does, too.

I walk across the room to the CD player and press "Play." Piano. George Winston. *Yes.*

Matt, a senior student and a published poet, walks in without a word and leaves a poem on the books atop my desk that serve as my "In" box. I've been his primary poetry editor this year. Work is stacked up, so I won't get to his poem until seven tomorrow morning. The hour before school begins is my prime editing and responding time.

Next, it's time for me to check on the kids around the building. I stride down the corridor and stop by Jim Buley's room, giving a nod to let him know I'm out on patrol. We frequently cover each other's class. In the media center, the two Writing Center editors on duty are chitchatting at the teacher's desk. I don't smile. They shuffle papers nervously. Once I pass, they begin to chat again. There's no editing business at the moment, but I take their roles seriously.

Of the six 109ers who came to the Writing Center, five are on computers. The sixth, Jason, is in the corner of the library with his girlfriend. I eye him down, and he waves, signaling one more minute. Jason gets his work done in good order. No problem there. As I walk out, I pause at the Writing Center desk.

"It'd be good if you'd walk around and see if anyone needs help," I say.

"We did that five minutes ago," says Jeff.

"We don't want to keep bugging them," says Melissa.

"You're right," I say.

Upstairs in the 213 computer room, the clicking of computer keys and the right count of my students assure me things are fine. Back to 109.

There, Peter has crashed on the couch with the book on his face. By reading his journal two weeks ago, I discovered his home life is a disaster because his parents split up. He's been living with his twenty-year-old sister. She's a partier. Peter's in trouble. I make a mental note to talk with him this week. For now, I suspect he needs his sleep.

I pick up my stack of mail and begin tearing open the pieces that aren't trying to sell me stuff. Jamie has written a long letter from Bates College. Halfway through my reading of the letter, Jason returns to the room and swats Peter's feet off the other side of the couch so he can sit in comfort.

Barb returns from the art room and comes directly to my desk. "I'm working today and tomorrow after school on my airbrush. It's going to be so cool. Ms. Wing and I came up with some good ideas. I can present next class."

I smile. "Great. One less for next Friday."

Joey overhears us. "Hey, I've almost got mine done. I can present next class, too."

"Well, okay," I cheer.

Jim pops by my doorway and waves as he heads out to the media center.

I pick up Jamie's letter from Bates and move to the door so I can listen in on Jim's students.

Great news! Jamie's got a job writing for the Bates student newspaper.

10:16 A.M.

About seventy more minutes of class. Three more trips to the computer room and Writing Center. Four more book recommendations. One card written to Jamie. Five emails answered, three to former students away at college, one to my friend Suzie in Alaska, and one to my brother Allen about Emily Dickinson. One Nutri-Grain bar scoffed down. A chuckle shared with my Spanish teaching friend Cheryl. One phone call taken. Finish up a class letter on relationships and think about our upcoming discussion. Check out the rest of the snail mail. My friend Jerry pops by with his daily words of wisdom. Chat with four students about portfolio stuff. Search for my favorite black felt-tipped pen in the upper drawer of my desk. Promise to clean the upper drawer of my desk.

Classroom Themes

In a portfolio pedagogy, themes provide a common thread that helps build a classroom community. In the first quarter of this year our class discussions focused on diversity, boredom, and ethics. The theme of "boredom" came out of our discussions on diversity and difference. In some classes we spent weeks discussing "ethics," while in other classes we virtually ignored it. In the end, students represented these themes in some fashion in their portfolios, from a short story on a gay high school student to "101 Ways to Defeat Boredom in Rumford, Maine."

I don't tell the students how to represent the themes in their papers, projects, or presentations. Nor do I tell them which genre to employ. These decisions are a part of their learning. I do, in passing, make suggestions in class as we discuss the theme. I confer individually with the students to help look at the possibilities. I also supply a variety of models. Some examples are by former students, some are by me in the form of class letters, and others come from absolutely every source imaginable. (And with our Internet connection, those sources are endless.) Ultimately, what my student colleagues write is their decision. Again, variety is the key.

Sometimes I offer several themes, and as a class we select one. At other times I jump right into a discussion on a particular theme that I choose. Finally, there are times when students develop the theme.

"Balance" is frequently the yearlong theme in Room 109. It provides endless jumping-off places. Here are a few examples of the many subthemes that surface from our discussions and studies:

- Exploring the summer and winter minds with Wallace Stevens
        winter mind=objectivity   summer mind=subjectivity

- What it is to be a woman (womyn) and what it is to be a man

- Infinity—balancing the known with the unknown

- Variety of sentence structures for creating sound balance

- Making meaning—chaos, form, and order with Wallace Stevens, E. A. Robinson, Robert Frost, and others

- Word choice and variety

- The balance within a novel, short story, poem, or essay

- Humor: Does it provide balance?

- Creative writing across the curriculum; math and science poems

- Finding balance as a learner: Rethinking our schools

- Studies on diversity and difference: Is a good world a balanced world?

- How history balances our lives

- Quantum physics and poetry

- How language influences our actions and thoughts

- Learning: If "all knowledge is provisional" (Barnes 1988), how do we go on learning?

- The balanced student: Learning through teaching

- *Hamlet* and *Macbeth*: Balanced plays with unbalanced characters?

Each of these subthemes is broken down again into more specific subject areas by individual students. In other words, the students personalize them. August writes about being a mother and how her son Kyle creates both balance and imbalance in her life. One of her projects has baby items, including a tiny baseball cap and a small toy car dangling from the thick cardboard poster. When she introduces the work to her classmates, August explains that the project symbolizes balance, love, and motherhood.

Kevin writes how "basketball" balances his life. He reads Steve Alford's *Playing for Knight* and discusses how Indiana's coach Bobby Knight finds his own personal balance. Kevin writes another essay about the different coaches he's enjoyed or "survived" in his athletic career. (I coached him in soccer. Yes, he was kind.)

Different students, different interests, different focuses, yet linked by common themes. One way to create a responsive classroom society.

Another Class: Class Discussions and the Genesis of a Theme

"Journals," I announce.

A few groans.

They take out their journal notebooks, a piece of composition paper, or, once in a while, a notebook computer. Their faces reflect a variety of expressions; indifference seems to be the most common. I understand. Sometimes even fun gets old. I'm not a magician, just a guy with a story to tell. I've saved this one until we have come to know each other fairly well. March or April—mud season in Maine, the doldrums of the school year.

"This is a true story. It happened at Lake Placid six years ago." They quiet. I don't tell stories for journals too often, and I suspect something in the sound of my voice alerts them.

"I was coaching at the New England cross-country ski championships. One of my racers was standing in the arena watching the boys race. All of a sudden the kid next to her just collapses. She bends down. Shakes him. He doesn't move. He's not breathing."

Now, most of their eyes are on me. I pause. Walk halfway around the circle of desks. Silence. Not a word. It's one of *those* moments all teachers experience once in a great while.

I continue. "Tammy does all the stuff you're supposed to do when something like this happens. Shake and shout. Clear the air passage. Tilt the head back and begin CPR."

"We just learned that in P.E.," whispers John.

"Word spreads around the arena. Another coach shouts and asks me to find Dr. Grover. His son is one of my racers. In the meantime, two other doctors arrive and take over the CPR."

This is all very real to me as I speak to my students. I can see the small crowd around the lifeless boy, and just to the left, every fifteen seconds, another racer takes off into the woods of Mt. Van Hovenberg, site of the 1980 Winter Olympics. I'll never forget the scene: powerful young athletes tearing off in championship style and, not more than ten yards away, a young skier from Vermont lying lifeless in the snow.

"Tammy stood by and watched the doctors work on the boy. After she had caught her own breath, she began to sense that something was wrong. And it was. The doctors weren't doing the CPR right."

A barrage of questions. I raise my hand.

"You've got to understand that Tammy was certified in CPR; she knew how to do it. But what could she do? She was sixteen and these two doctors . . . well, that's just it. They were doctors."

"How do you know *she* was right?" asks one boy.

"Good question," I admit, and walk around the circle to the other side. "Dr. Grover and an emergency room nurse came to help out. They watched the two doctors—it only took them a moment to see that it wasn't right. They immediately took over."

Silence. To my students this is not one of my gimmicky journal ideas like "Why do stores that are open twenty-four hours a day, 365 days a year have locks on the doors?" I can see them struggling.

"The ambulance came. And as if everything else wasn't bad enough, the defibrillator didn't work. The boy died."

I wait for a moment while my students' eyes settle. "I learned later that the boy had suffered a heart attack and that the autopsy results showed that he'd had others. His heart was weak and damaged—an 'anomaly,' they called it. Nothing would have saved him."

"How could doctors screw up CPR?" asks Peter, indignantly.

"I asked that, too. These two physicians weren't emergency room doctors. They did internal medicine. In their practices they don't do CPR, so they just did the best they could."

"Yes, but they must have learned it," insisted Peter.

"I'm sure. But we forget things we don't use."

"That's no excuse," says Becky, her red hair seeming to sharpen her words.

"I'd sue them," snaps Fred. Others agree.

"What do you want us to write about?" asks John.

Finally, the question. "I'd like you to tell me what you would have done. Would you have said something to the doctors? Would you have said, 'You're doing that wrong'?" I wait another moment. "What would you have done?"

They look at me briefly. Some drop their heads to write. Others grimace. A few make those little groaning noises that go along with hard thinking. They want to say the right thing. They want to say that they'd be brave enough to step in and speak up. But I know, and so do they.

I need to help them. "I know one thing for sure: At sixteen years old, I would not have said a word. I might have even run away."

They're relieved.

"I still can't believe they didn't know how to do it," says Becky.

"I know what you mean. At first, I couldn't understand either. But the way I look at it now is that they did their best. What more can we ask? So, take some time and think about what you would have done. Or, if you like, write about authority and how it affects us."

"I wouldn't have said anything," says Jen.

"Me neither," admits David.

Most agree with them. Even with their admissions, they look empty and defeated.

I say, "Someone gave me a button a few years ago. It says, 'Question Authority.' I try, but it's not easy."

"Mr. Kent, would you say something to the doctors now?" asks Becky.

Almost every time I offer this journal entry, someone asks. Every time, I answer the same way.

"I'm not sure."

Neither are they.

Where do we go after this journal entry? It depends on the class. Often, the kids talk animatedly about the authorities that rule their lives: parents, teachers, older students, bosses, and girlfriends/ boyfriends. From these discussions come a variety of papers, art projects, or presentations. Some kids seek out books on the subject; others might write the one journal entry on "obedience to authority" and end it there. Some interview parents, principals, police officers, and doctors; others do nothing. One or two might spend their entire quarter studying aspects of authority; one or two others might sit on the couch and play cards. Almost always, the choice is theirs.

My role in all of this? Sometimes I usher in certain concepts and ideas through the Socratic method. Other times, after reading the interest level of the class, I let go. Indeed, it is a balancing act. One thing's for sure, there's never a dull moment.

Developing Themes and Sharing Ideas: Class Letters

I write class letters to my students frequently. These letters introduce themes as well as help me think about those we have selected to study. It's important for my students to see me—a writer, thinker, and student—work and struggle with these ideas right alongside of them. This sharing helps build a collegial atmosphere.

Another reason for writing class letters involves the development of a student's writing voice. Being able to identify another writer's voice is an important step toward realizing our own. By the end of the year, not only have my students read twenty or thirty class letters and six or more personal letters from me, many have also read my novels. "Mr. Kent, I read your book. I can hear *you* in it."

I also find these letters helpful as a way of reinforcing my writing instruction. I might focus on parallel construction or the elimination of passive voice. The letters are especially useful for introducing or emphasizing punctuation. During class when we go over the letter, I will point out the usage. A lesson here, a lesson there. Always as authentic as I can make it.

Finally, I write class letters for the sheer joy of writing.

Once a year we analyze a film. Two of my favorites are (the 1970s classic) *Harold and Maude* and (the more recent) *What's Eating Gilbert Grape?*

My Dear Students,
    I hope you have enjoyed the production of *What's Eating Gilbert Grape?* I have, over and over again. I'm engaged by Arnie, his smile, his innocence, his humor. He makes me laugh. What a good guy. All of us would enjoy having such a brother or a friend. Some of us do.
    I'm also interested in the struggles of a small-town American family. I didn't feel for Gilbert as much as I felt for the Grape family as a whole. Gilbert says at the beginning of the movie that "Endora is like dancing to no music." The thing is, we can dance without music if we have imagination *and* if we have the right partner. For me,

Gilbert has control of his own dance. He's made his choices, music or not.

Each character in this movie is a study. I suspect all of you could write a short paper on most of them. For me, however, it's the continual reference to food that eats at me. (Sorry about that!) Did you notice that in almost every scene someone is eating? Did you notice the constant conversation about food, from Burger Barn to greasy bacon, from melting ice cream to the sexual rituals of the praying mantis? Did you notice that food even eclipsed Mr. Carver's funeral as the good old Burger Barn—much to Arnie's delight— arrived during the service? And what of the title? *What's EATING Gilbert GRAPE?* Food, food, food.

I also enjoyed the subtleties in the movie. The foreshadowing is strong throughout. We hear the undertaker talking about making "harmless jokes" about "particularly grotesque bodies" when they are on the slab in the funeral home. In the end, the Grapes didn't want their morbidly obese mom to be the object of ridicule after her death. Sadly, of course, she was. Remember the police radio? "It'll take the National Guard to get her out of there."

We also hear the undertaker talking about the ultimate joke played on people each day: One moment we're enjoying life, and the next day we're dead. At that very moment in the movie, the camera pans over to the Carvers as they *eat* breakfast. A couple of days later Mr. Carver has a heart attack and falls dead into the swimming pool that his kids so desperately wanted. Did you notice the precursor to all of this was Mrs. Carver burning the cookies in the oven? Food, food, food. Why?

And there are so many other thoughts to develop:

- What of the water tower? What does it symbolize? Could it be *escape?*

- What of the trailers coming through town?

- What of the small-town grocery and the gigantic Food Land? (Food again!)

- "I could go at any time," says Arnie. Yet it's Mr. Carver, a healthy looking, relatively young man with a young wife and little boys, who dies.

- After her husband's funeral, Mrs. Carver says to her sons, "You can have anything you want" in the store. "You can have candy if you want," says Arnie.

- "I made up the bed for you, Momma," says her daughter. Mrs. Grape returns, "I'm happy right where I am." Arnie screaming to Gilbert: "We're not going anywhere! We're not going anywhere!"

- Humor plays a large role in this movie. Gilbert lets the neighborhood kids get a good look at the "beached whale." Yet, at the same time, Gilbert is particularly careful (sensitive?) not to let his 400- to 500-pound mother know that they are shoring up the weakening floor. In another scene, Gilbert jokes, "My mother is attached to the house. She's wedged in."

- Near the end of the movie, Mrs. Carver says, "I could have had any man in this town, but I chose you." "Why?" asks Gilbert. "Because I knew you'd always be there," she answers.

- And what of the town's name—Endora?

There's some fun to be had with this movie. Find a theme or a character to develop, and go with it. **Don't be care-full** . . . be reckless, bold, and far-reaching in your thinking. There's much to be said for *wild minds*.

As always, YLET,
Richard Kent

5

Coaching Writers in a Portfolio Classroom

What a child writes is of the same order as what the poet or novelist writes and valid for the same reasons.
James Britton

During Christmas vacation and The other Vacation's. On Christmas eve morning me and my dad went up in the woods to go make a couple of hitches. When we got there we tried to start up the skitter after a while we got it started we put the chokechains on the back of the skitter. After I got done putting the chokechains on I put my chap's on and got onto the skitter and went to go get a hitch of tree's. When my dad cut's down tree's I have to hitch them up and if I feel like I limb the tree's sometimes. Around 12:00 we ate lunch and headed back up to get more hitches of wood when we went back down to the yard the pulp truck was there so I unhooked the log's and went to park the skitter. About 3 minutes later my dad's boss showed up. We had to pull the pulp truck up into the yard. When we got it up there we un hooked the pulp truck from the skitter and he started loading the truck up. My dad was up in the back of the trucks body piling the wood right so it would 'nt fall out. My dad's boss went to start up the skitter to fuel it up and oil it. the fuel was down in his truck so he brough the skitter down there and fueled it up. When we got done we parked the skitter by my dad's truck well not to close. When we got done loading the pulp truck we picked up to go home when we got home we changed and I went down stairs to go see what my grandfather was doing he said nothing so I went out side and Chris came over and we went on the back trail to clean the tree's out of the way we're not done yet. When we have time we're going to finish it When I got home we went to a friends house his name is Leelin he is probably 56 years old he is a real friend to us. When we went home me and Chris played Super Tecmo Bowl and Street Fighter II. After I went home and ate supper. And after I went down stairs because we had a Christmas eve party my aunts and uncles and all of my cousins and my grandparents. Well it was there house we had it in I live up stairs from them. We have a it every year down there. After I went up stairs because we had company to then we had a little Christmas ever party to my parents went out and I went to East Andover with my grandmother to go get my cousins Regine 10 years old and my other cousin Eric 7 years old. I stayed down down my grandparent's house for the night. The next me Eric, and my other cousin Robert. A week later I went up in the woods with my dad and my grandfather when we got up there we tried to start up the skitter but it wouldn't start so my dad said forget it so we cut some boat wood up and loaded up the three trucks I had one my dad had one and my grandfather had his well I had my grandfathers scout four wheel drive. After we got done loading up the trucks we got in them and headed for home we drove the galond pond road over to my house the when I got home I seen my cousin Robbie running back and forth over to my uncles house across the road from my cousins house and my uncle lives next door to me. Anyway I went over to see what was wrong I went into the house and it was full of smoke so I called the fire Department because it was a fire. Anyway the house burnt flat down I helped hold the water hose. What a New Year he had huh. Right now they are making out good. Anyway he had good Insurance. After it was done I went home and brought up wood and ate and them I left

The
End
Peter Stryker

Peter's Story: Another Way of Seeing

When I first began to read Peter's story, the corrector in me surfaced. I scoffed at the title and how it ran into the text. The single spacing annoyed me. I began inserting commas, changing constructions, and figuring out how I could fix all of the run-ons.

I'm not sure exactly what made me stop dead in my correcting tracks. Part of it must have been the guilt I felt for marking up

Peter's story without his permission, a courtesy I automatically afforded all writers. *Did I take Peter's writing less seriously because he was a special education student?*

Then the echoes from the previous summer studying with Michael Armstrong. "How do we represent to children the quality and potential of their thinking? The first requirement is to recognize the authority of children's texts."

The authority of children's texts.

Peter's teacher, John Jamison, handed me the story early one morning. "Got any suggestions?" I sensed John's frustration, but admired his patience and his gentle manner. He believed in his students; he respected them.

Again, Michael's voice cut through the haze. "To teach writing, in a sense, is a way of teaching people to tell the stories of their lives" (1992). I put the pencil down and started to read Peter's story again, from the beginning. This time I read like a writer, a coach, and a caring friend. I looked for the power and the potentiality of Peter's story.

I didn't have to look far.

Dear John,

Peter's retelling of his holiday is fascinating. The expressive nature of the piece makes it most engaging. There are no pretensions, no ambiguities, and nothing self-conscious about the writing . . . what we see is what we get. The honesty behind such a piece is rich, warm, and refreshing—I felt as if I were being invited into Peter's family and into his life. At the end I felt trusted and honored to have been included.

Peter is most detailed in his opening few lines about his Christmas Eve work with his "dad" and the "skitter." From his writing I feel a sense of understanding and maturity on Peter's behalf when it comes to work in the woods. In the woods Peter is capable, confident, and knowledgeable. There, he would be *my* teacher.

It's obvious through his retelling that Peter is trusted by his father. Their relationship sounds wonderful—father and son working together in the woods—what a healthy and sound relationship to read about. I don't hear anything about Peter being ordered into the woods to work with his father: ". . . me and my dad went up in the woods to go make a couple of hitches."

Peter's voice throughout is even tempered and kind. He never assumes, he never pushes. What I truly loved was that the "work" didn't sound like labor. To the contrary, Peter and his dad joined in celebration of sorts . . . listen to the relationship:

"When we got done we parked the skitter by my dad's truck well not to close. When we got done loading the pulp truck we picked up to go home when we got home we changed . . ."

For most of this expressive piece, Peter is deeply involved in relationship. He talks about himself briefly, but the mainstay of his writing is involved with others. People matter to Peter.

". . . we went to a friends house his name is Leelin he is probably 56 years old he is a real friend to us."

The more I read the piece, the deeper I listen to Peter, the more I come to know how wonderfully warm he is as a person. He identifies his cousins by name and age. This detail shows respect for the reader and, undoubtedly, for his cousins. They're not just names.

The precision of Peter's description brings life to the piece. It's not just a truck, it's a "scout four wheel drive." It's not simply Nintendo, it's "Super Tecmo Bowl and Street Fighter II." It's not wood, it's "boat wood." Detail after detail shows Peter's force as an author and as a storyteller. In its purest form, this writing has a kind of brilliance within it that the average reader might lose if bothered by the lack of "correctness."

If I were to grade the variety of sentence structures in this piece, Peter would receive high marks. His writing is rich with diversity—a pleasant combination of variety. Many young adult writers struggle getting beyond noun-verb-complement sentence structures. Peter has avoided the trap of "I went to the woods . . . I drove the skidder . . . I ate lunch."

His is an active piece that is filled with phrases and clauses and literary techniques that usher the reader into and through the story. Listen:

"When we went home . . ."

"On Christmas eve morning . . ."

"Anyway I went over . . ."

"Well, it was there house . . ."

"A week later I went up . . ."

In the last few lines we hear the conclusion building. The house didn't just burn, "the house burnt flat down and I helped hold the water hose." Details, always details. And then the personal side—back to considering the reader: "What a New Year he had huh." He speaks directly to us. Again, no pretension, no showboating, no melodrama.

Peter's piece ends simply and honestly. "After it was done I went home and brought up wood and ate and them I left . . ."

Peter is an author. He has developed an engaging story that skillfully takes the listener through a ten day period with the kind of detail that all fine writers aspire to. Once the reader allows him- or herself to get beyond the technical differences of Peter's style compared to what most consider as acceptable, this young man's writing creates music with its rich and wonderfully composed descriptive passages.

Warmly,
Rich

"Now I see," said John.
So did I.

Peter wrote many stories that year. The next one had the same number of "grammaticals" as his Christmas story, but it was double spaced. John had convinced him of that. When Peter brought it to me to read, I took a chance.

"This is really interesting. I like it as much as your Christmas story. I'm curious about one thing, though. Listen to this." I read him the first line that had a missing word.

"Duh!" he sounded, slapping his forehead in mock disgust. "Left out a word."

"After I write something it helps me to read my stuff out loud," I explained. "I catch the little mistakes."

Both John and I continued to encourage Peter. He loved coming across the hallway to share his stories with me. He especially enjoyed coming in when my room was full of students. It was not difficult to figure out why. Peter suffered from *fetal alcohol syndrome* (FAS). All his life he had been relegated to special education. Now, his work—and, in a real sense, *he*—had busted loose.

Peter never seemed inhibited when he came to visit. Each new story showed a bit of growth. Each had the sign of an author struggling to find those "best" words. In time, he began to edit pieces with Mr. Jamison and keep the drafts in a folder. Whenever I saw him—in the hallways, down in the cafeteria, at sporting events—Peter would talk about his writing. "I'm doing one on the speedway up at Oxford." "I'm writing about snow machining with my uncle and cousins."

Talking with Peter about his writing had the same feel as talking with my adult writer friends. "I get stuck here after I tell about winning the race." "Sometimes the words don't come." Unlike many of my student writers, Peter's focus stayed on the story. We never diverted, chatting about the Red Sox or Celtics, spring break or summer plans. It was the story, plain and simple. *His story.*

If I offered even the smallest suggestion about content, Peter would adamantly reject it. He had a definite sense of the story because he had lived it. "I can't say that. That's not the way it happened."

Most times when I passed his room and glanced in, Peter sat poised at the computer, composing. In every sense of the word, he lived a writer's life. He kept regular hours. He had an editor, a readership, and a portfolio of work. He always talked story: the essence of plot, the development of character, the elusiveness of words. Peter possessed a powerful presence as a writer.

John continually complimented me on my work with Peter. However, it didn't take long to find out exactly who, besides Peter himself, deserved credit.

After reading his third story (he cranked out two a week), I called a friend at the middle school who worked in special education. I wanted to know Peter's history as a writer. His file in the high school office had a wad of papers on disciplinary actions and a series of documentation about his FAS diagnosis, but no significant writing samples.

My friend's words are still with me: "Peter never wrote more than three lines in middle school."

Epilogue

At the end of the year, John Jamison packed up the contents of his desk and his country home. He moved to the Pacific Northwest, where he teaches today. During the last few weeks of the year, John came into my room a number of times. Before leaving, he spoke passionately out of concern for his students. "I don't think people see what I see in these kids. They have so much to offer."

The following August, I handed the new teacher Peter's portfolio. "I thought you'd find Peter's stories fascinating. Let me know if there's anything I can do to help."

She smiled. "Oh great. I can't wait to read them."

That year, Peter stopped writing altogether. The new teacher lost the collection of Peter's stories, and later, she lost her job.

Being a Writing Coach

I cannot be the primary editor for my 120 students when they are writing twenty papers a year. (It feels so good to be able to say that and not feel an iota of guilt.)

Before portfolios, I always took a "set of papers" home with me at night to "correct." I read and marked every draft of every student's paper. I don't do that now. Being my students' primary editor meant assigning less writing, requiring fewer drafts, and still staying up past the late night news. Portfolios have helped me resolve this dilemma and have helped my students become better writers, editors, and thinkers.

I do work one on one with students, especially when we compose poetry. I also personally edit cover letters for job applications or college admissions essays. But I am no longer a day-to-day corrector. I don't spend my time doing things that Writing Center editors, classmates, *keepers*, or computers can do. I have a different role. I am a writing coach.

Think of the effort involved in sustaining the dialogue required of a part-time editor who has to work with 120 writers and what is now a minimum of twelve thousand pages of manuscript a year. I say "part time" because writing is only one of my many responsibilities as a high school language arts teacher. Whether hiking up the side of a mountain on a Sunday morning to visit a "dig site" or writing recommendations, my days are filled with the lives of young people.

Before portfolios, my students wrote half as much as they do now. There was some peer editing going on, but Mr. Kent usually dominated the scene. With portfolios, my young colleagues regularly produce four to eight drafts for each of their formal papers. With that volume of work, I have found that a crucial part of a student's development as a writer is learning to find a competent editor and to establish a working relationship. This is a skill that a person will use for a lifetime. The searching, negotiating, discussing, and decision making while working with an editor is the real stuff of writing.

Students' primary editors are classmates, Writing Center staffers, other teachers, *keepers*, and various computer programs. My major role as a writing coach in Room 109 is to read and analyze the students' collected work in their quarterly portfolios. Once examined, I make specific comments that will help each student move toward another level of competency. Commenting on an archive of writing has made me a different kind of editor and certainly more effective. Truly, it's a luxury to have a large body of work to scrutinize.

Coaching Ryan

In his junior year, Ryan kept goal for our championship soccer team and wore a smile that wouldn't quit. His first-quarter portfolio contained rich detailed thinking and interesting personal commentaries. His projects were highlighted by a riotous video presentation that he, Chad, and Adam produced on the history of The Doors and a six-foot-long circa 1920 biplane for St. Exupery's *Wind, Sand and Stars.* He and Jeff, who happened to be the last-line defender on our soccer team, constructed the plane out of wire coat hangers. It still hangs from the ceiling of my classroom.

In reading Ryan's portfolio, some one hundred pages of manuscript, I recognized a weakness—long, chatty sentences—that surfaced in both his highly edited formal papers and his journals. The "what" of his papers depicted an intelligent young man; the "how" rambled on. In my portfolio letter to him, I expressed my concern.

In a follow-up talk at the beginning of the second quarter, we discussed my observation further. I suggested a mixture of sentence constructions as well as a variety of sentence lengths. Other recommendations included reading his work aloud for a "sound edit" and explaining the problem to his editors so that they might key in on it. Finally, I offered to edit one of his papers to help him work on this problem. That never happened.

Interestingly, in her *keeper* letter for the first-quarter portfolio, Ryan's mom commented that "he still writes like he talks and sometimes that doesn't flow well." During parent conferences we discussed Ryan's rambling style.

Here's a portion of my second-quarter letter to him nine weeks later:

> Guess what? Your writing has improved. Your long-winded, chatty lines have been transformed into well balanced sentences. I noticed how you picked which editors' comments to use and which to pass by. Quite mature. A "good see" in the writing world.

Ryan's writing changed significantly, and yet I never edited one of his papers. I did, however, coach him. And along with his editors' advice, Ryan moved to another level.

The Trouble with *Corrector* Editing

Since becoming a teacher researcher by looking closely at my practice, I have made some interesting discoveries. One of those discoveries involves a major problem in the teaching of writing and editing. I call it *corrector editing.* Simply stated, corrector editing happens when an editor rewrites entire sentences—or paragraphs—of an author's manuscript.

Back when I attempted to act as the primary editor for all of my students, almost every comment or suggestion I made they took as the gospel. Why? Partly because as their teacher and a writer myself, they trusted me. Partly because it relieved their struggles as a writer by eliminating difficult decisions. Finally, and sadly enough, my students seemed more focused on grades and pleasing me than on being good writers with reasonable habits. In all of this, I was an enabler as well as a prisoner of time.

The result? My students allowed *and* encouraged me to make the crucial writing decisions for them; in fact, they used my suggestions carte blanche. In the end, they did little generative thinking during revision.

Indeed, *corrector editing* eliminates (bypasses) part of the writer's process. I see this each and every day; in fact, I used to do this each and every day. Traditionally, schools have promoted this kind of writing and editing; it is a byproduct of an archaic time schedule and large class sizes. When the ratio is 120 to 1, teachers and students don't have the time to form genuine writer and editor relationships.

I have especially noticed this kind of editing on the part of *keepers.* A look at many of my students' rough drafts shows endless cross-outs and replacements. Entire paragraphs have been rewritten by well-meaning adults. This kind of revision only makes sense because these adults are products of a system that promoted correction and getting it right fast. Indeed, the writing process was misunderstood.

What we have learned about the writing process over the years includes an understanding of revision and the importance of editors. We know that effective editors hint, suggest, and question; they make the writing and editing process a journey of discovery. On the other hand, correctors tell, change, and delete; this kind of relationship verges on coauthorship and is every bit a forced march.

It's clear. Fixing someone's text isn't editing, and eliminating the decision-making side of composing isn't writing. One role of a teacher in portfolio pedagogy is working hard to get the word out to editors: Please don't rewrite the paper for the author. Still, it's an on-going battle. Another role of the teacher is the excruciating act of leaving student writers alone to discover on their own.

With the freedom to select their own editors—be they Writing Center staffers or their Aunt Betty—students create the needed time for edits that are journeys of a process. As a writing coach, I am able to come along for the ride. Some days I'm in the back seat; other days I ride shotgun. Every once in a while I take the wheel.

Minilessons

In 109, grammar and spelling are addressed on a daily basis in the context of the editing process. When a student composes five papers per quarter and revises those five papers up to eight times with an editor, a lot of conversation about grammar, spelling, diction, sound quality, and the nitty-gritty of writing takes place. Yet, sometimes my students need more.

This year after reading and responding to the 117 first-quarter portfolios, commas seemed to be a bugaboo amongst many of my students. As a result, I added a three-day minilesson on the six comma rules from Teresa Ferster Glazier's *The Least You Should Know About English*. During the year, the same happened with semicolons and punctuating dialogue. And yes, I might give them a few work sheets to crunch through, though the difference is that we create our own work sheets. I might also take a page out of something I've written and eliminate all the commas or quotation marks.

Generally, I spend between twenty and forty minutes during three consecutive classes presenting minilessons. It's kind of a fun time for the kids. They don't often see me performing this way—or as Julie blurted out, "You're acting like a regular teacher, Mr. Kent!" (Go figure, Julie.)

I've also discovered that my students pick up lessons in punctuation, diction, and construction—the stuff of writing—by reading my class letters and portfolio responses. Often, I will point out usage in a parenthetical statement in the midst of a class letter. (Notice how the introductory word "often" is followed by a comma.) Or, I might bring up certain constructions in class after they've had a chance to read my letter. Another thing I've noticed, if I use ellipses in my letters, sure enough, kids begin to use them. If I use the words "quintessential" or "oxymoronic," they do too. All of this points out yet again the power we teachers wield as models.

In keeping with our yearlong theme, I continually talk about their writing in terms of *balance.* Here are some of the most common points I make when I confer with or write to my students about their writing. I also stress these points throughout the year during mini-lessons. And finally, these points guide the editors of the Writing Center as they work with their clients.

- Vary the length of your sentences.

- Vary the construction of your sentences.

- Watch your paragraphs: Too long or too short could spell a problem.

- Don't overuse uncommon words like *idiosyncratic* or *flamboyant.*

- Use active voice and avoid the verb *to be.*

- Avoid telling us "she was angry." Show us her "gritted teeth and reddening face."

- In short stories, let the characters do the talking. We want to hear their voices.

- Use semicolons sparingly.

- Rarely use exclamation points. Let your words create the excitement.

- Use complete sentences ninety-nine percent of the time.

- Look at your piece to see that you have a well-developed beginning, middle, and ending.

- Try using parallel construction. It adds rhythm to your writing.

- Read your writing aloud, preferably to someone else.

Some minilessons take just a few minutes to present. When discussing passive voice, for example, I ask students to take out a formal paper from the previous quarter's portfolio. "Circle every *was, were, is,* or *are* in your paper," I say. "Now see if you can rewrite some of these sentences using active verbs." I hand out a sheet with a short list of active verbs:

administered	droop	climb	contributed
pierce	hum	created	celebrate
wonder	erase	developed	advocate
weave	grind	offend	emerge
wrap	reflect	grasp	quiver
encourage	need	drone	flounder
collapse	urge	surmise	plead
split	burst	petition	trust

Reconstructing pieces of work they have written helps them see the potential of their own writing. And, as we know, active voice helps our writing sing.

Two remarkable books have helped validate my thinking and further shape my understanding of the teaching of writing: Tom Romano's *Clearing the Way: Working with Teenage Writers* and Nancie Atwell's *In the Middle: Writing, Reading, and Learning with Adolescents.*

Additionally, *Teaching Writing as Reflective Practice* by George Hillocks, Jr., has helped me link the theoretical with actual classroom practice.

Writing Ourselves: Developing a Base of the Expressive

One focus of the 109 portfolio is to insure my students build a large foundation of expressive writing (e.g., journals, letters, diaries, learning logs). Of the three categories of writing, including transactional (e.g., term papers, reports, essays) and poetic (e.g., fiction, poetry, drama, and songs), the expressive "is crucial for trying out and coming to terms with new ideas" (Martin 1991).

> Expressive writing enables children to make sense for themselves of what they have seen or read or done or talked about by composing it for themselves in their own words. Thus expressive writing is fundamental to learning—in any subject matter—because it enables children to internalize knowledge, to make it part of themselves, by putting it together in their own terms. (Atwater 1981)

Since this type of writing is closest to our thinking process—to ourselves—large amounts of first-draft expressive writing help my student colleagues develop their writing voices while eliminating the "blank computer screen" syndrome.

> *After portfolios, I'll never be afraid of* how much *I have to write ever again.*
> Andrea G., a sophomore

On the first day of school when I assign the five-page autobiographical sketch due the very next class, bulging eyes, gasps, and sighs ripple through the classroom. At the end of the year when I hand out the final reflection, a piece that often results in twenty to thirty pages of thoughtful writing, there's rarely a whisper. I love to witness the difference.

For me, the expressive is like distance training for an athlete. The huge base of writing required in a 109 portfolio provides a firm foundation from which to grow and perform with power and precision. In writing, as in dance or sports or knitting, managed sustained practice makes us better.

In addition, writing ourselves—being able to speak about our lives, our views, and our world vision in our own language (e.g., the way a book touches us, the purpose in our eyes of certain math exercises, and the manner in which we may personally apply certain scientific principles)—is crucial for cognition. It is also essential in terms of how students view the importance of certain school work. "How is this exercise relevant to me and my world?" Discovering our own voices and our ability to create meaning within the context of our world vision is a matter of primary importance to learners.

At Bread Loaf I learned that an increased emphasis on expressive writing is needed across the disciplines. In fact, James Britton and his colleagues proclaimed the expressive as the base from which all writing and thinking begins. Furthermore, research by the Britton team showed a neglect of expressive writing in schools.

Once I learned about this neglect, we organized a schoolwide investigation. The Writing Center editors of Mountain Valley High School conducted a research project amongst staff and students to ascertain the amounts and types of writing accomplished across the curriculum in our school. The results revealed that the expressive accounted for only six percent of the writing in the school. Eighty-two percent was transactional, and twelve percent was poetic.

Randall Freisinger (1982) believes that "excessive reliance on the transactional function of language may be substantially responsible for our students' inability to think critically and independently . . . Product oriented, transactional language promotes closure" (9).

In the past, schools ignored this function of language and learning across the disciplines. But now . . .

"Mr. Kent, have you been talking to Mr. Todd?" asks Katie, arms folded, face stern.

"What do you mean?"

"We're doing journals in math!"

I had *not* spoken with my math colleague Marshall Todd. He studied the research; and like other science, math, and technology teachers, he discovered the power and importance of the expressive through journal writing and learning logs. In the transactional world of science, technology, and math, "the expressive" helps our future scientists and mathematicians make meaning of concepts and connect to ideas.

As a result of my summer studies and the realization that "the expressive" helps students learn, I increased the yearly writing requirements in Room 109. Sixty to eighty journals per year became two hundred, and I quadrupled the amount of reflective writing. I also asked my students to write more letters to their classroom colleagues in response to individual pieces of writing, book projects, presentations, and entire portfolios.

One wonderful book to read on "the expressive" and other functions of writing is *Mostly About Writing: Selected Essays* by Nancy Martin (1983). Martin, Mr. Britton's longtime colleague and friend, has helped me see the process of writing more clearly. She has such a high respect for young people as readers and writers—as learners—that listening to her is a model for any teacher.

The Confusion over First-Draft, Expressive Writing

We write for different purposes and, thus, in different ways.

An email message from the chair of English at a prestigious university states that "your going to hear from him in the futrue." Does the professor know the difference between "you're" and "your"? Absolutely. Does the chair of English know how to spell "future"? Without question. But when we use email our focus is on the message, the idea, and the immediacy of the response. If this same person were writing a position paper to the full faculty, would there be any misspelled words? No way.

A letter from a *keeper* at the front of his child's portfolio included this small comment: "What I find difficult to swallow is the lack of spelling and grammar skills in the free flowing journal entries" in Brian's portfolio.

My quick response focused on an analogy between alpine ski racing (the man is a former ski racer) and the various categories of writing. If you're not at all familiar with ski racing, you might flounder a bit with what's to follow. However, look at it this way: in whatever we do—be it ski racing, talking, dancing, writing, or making a meal—there are times when we are more formal than others. Then there are times when, for the sake of creativity and spontaneity, we simply *go for it* and disregard the formal rules.

Dear Roger,

I know exactly how you feel when you look at journals and see all the spelling problems and the other technical things. It has taken me time to learn to forget that stuff for the "greater good" of writing, thinking and freewriting. Think of it this way: Freewriting is much like free skiing for ski racers. The gates and the restrictions are taken away so the racer can blast down the slopes. During free skiing we learn the true meaning of being "on edge." Wonderfully creative and wild things happen to skiers when the barriers (gates) are removed. To be sure, experimentation is encouraged. Freewriting is an attempt to "free" the writer and to allow experimentation. If the writer is overly focused on spelling, commas, and paragraphing, my experience is a stiffer, less experimental kind of writing. Gate training is like 109's informal papers (one draft required) and a nationally sanctioned race is the equivalent of a formal, highly edited paper. To teach writing as well as skiing, you must allow for and introduce a bit of everything. As an alpine ski coach I took my skiers to *Tucks* [Tuckerman's Ravine on Mt. Washington, NH] so they could experiment with *the* steeps . . . I wanted them to have many experiences. In the end they became better skiers and better racers. This analogy might not quite touch all the questions you have, but I hope it lessens your concerns about freewrites. Thanks for posing the question; it gave me a chance to freewrite and explain journals through skiing . . . a fun exercise.

Best,
Rich

Assistant Writing Coaches

People ask me, "How do you manage with all the different levels of kids you have?" "How do you keep track of everything?"

I smile. All one has to do is to look through a collection of portfolios to know that I am *not* alone. I couldn't possibly be.

This acknowledgment page in the front of Matthew's portfolio says it best:

Thank You!

In the last nine weeks I have really hustled to put out another portfolio. Here it is! I would like to give special thanks to all of the people who have edited my papers and brought them out of the clutches of darkness into a brand new world.

Darcy Morse	Victor LeClaire
Wendy Michaud	Richard Todd
Katie Perry	Joey Labrecque
Brian Arsenault	April Glazier
Pam Saxton	Lindy Briggette
Lynn Smith	Jim McClean

Chrissy O'Brien
My mom and Tone (dear old dad)
. . . and, of course, Mr. Kent. He is the one who assigned this God forsaken thing.

Sincerely,
Matthew J. Glazier

From Writing Center editors to Mountain Valley staff members, from *keepers* to the senior citizen volunteers who come in after school, these are the assistant coaches, and the Room 109 portfolio would not exist without them.

Millie and Sarah's Coach, Mrs. Worthing

Millie and Sarah were not strong readers or writers when they arrived in 109. In truth, it took a while for them to trust words.

Their poems and essays remain some of my favorites for the joy and, at times, the power these writers derived from working with words and meanings.

Death is Destruction

Think about it!
Ovens with leftover bones
Executed bodies
All used for target practice
People in gas chambers
Holding their breath
Bodies all over the floor
Skinned from head to toe
Took fillings and shaved heads
Bulldozing over live people
Hearing screams underneath
Looking at dead carcasses
Seeing the tattoo numbers
on all the dead people
THOSE NAZI BASTARDS

Millie E.

And yet, I simply can't take the credit. Each day for most of the year, Millie and Sarah would announce, "We're going to try this out on Mrs. Worthing." They'd stride down the long first-floor hallway, laughing and carrying on, poems or essays in hand.

A while later they'd return, smug and smiling as if they'd landed a poem in *The New Yorker*.

"Mrs. Worthing loved it," declared Millie with a Scarletesque turn of the head.

Sarah, the quiet one, nodded vigorously.

Linda Worthing works in the media center as an aide. She recommends books, helps kids research, and surfs the Internet with the best of them. She's also one of the best editors and audiences any writer could ever ask for. Just ask Millie and Sarah.

Editing Parties

Sunday morning. The supermarket.

"Half your class was at my house last night," says Katherine, the mom of one of my students. We're standing in front of the iceberg lettuce.

"Why's that?" I ask, a bit startled.

"An editing party. What have you done to these kids?"

Pizza and soda flow freely, so do 109 papers. It happens around the seventh or eighth week of the quarter. I'd love to take credit for this one, but can you ever imagine an English teacher suggesting that his students meet on a Saturday night for a "party" to edit one another's papers? What are the chances?

Editing parties came out of the real need for these writers to receive feedback about their work. These parties have continued because the kids talk about the fun they have had. You can bet they're not one hundred percent focused on revising, but neither were one of my editors and I the last time we met (in fact, we hiked a mountain and spoke about Thoreau and soccer).

You'll know you've got a full-blown writers' workshop going when your students "party on down" with their writing on a Saturday evening.

The Writing Center

Most colleges and universities have writing centers, places where writers talk with fellow writers about their work. During my first year at Mountain Valley High School, I realized we needed a writing center much like the one my university students used at the University of Maine at Farmington. I approached my principal, Tom Rowe, with the idea, and his "go for it" sent me on my way.

I visited a learning center at a southern Maine high school and then solicited information and brochures from various college writing centers. Each month during the year, I reported to the English department on my findings; at the beginning my colleagues were quite supportive of the idea.

In June, after eight months of research and writing about the concept, the districtwide school board approved the idea on a trial basis. During the upcoming school year, I would direct the Writing Center and teach three English classes.

A political problem amongst some of my English colleagues surfaced when my teaching load was lessened to three classes. After the first year, I went back up to the standard five classes. This year, I added a sixth class.

In a high school that values and understands the power of *writing to learn,* a writing center director could be a full-time position. Without a writing center at Mountain Valley, I doubt my students would produce the quality or quantity of work that they do now. Directing the Writing Center is now an act of volunteerism on my part. In some ways it's not fair . . . but that's life teaching in a public school.

On average, I spend from seventy-five to one hundred hours per year on Writing Center work. Some of that time is spent in the summer corresponding with future editors. Some of my time is spent in developing brochures, training editors, keeping and publishing statistics, editing pieces of work, receiving visitors interested in high school writing centers, and fielding complaints from colleagues, students, and administrators. That's right, even though I am a volunteer, as director I still take the flak.

Recruiting Wendy: The Role of a Writing Center Editor

Exactly what do the editors do? Here's a letter to a prospective Writing Center editor that paints a picture of the job:

Dear Wendy,
    You have been recommended to me by several people, both student and faculty colleagues. I am always searching for students who would enjoy working as student editors in the Writing Center.

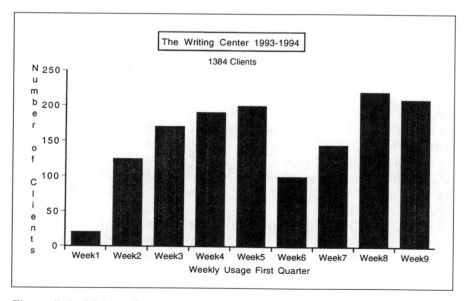

Figure 5–1. Writing Center Client Chart

The Writing Center
at
Mountain Valley High School

Editor's Sheet

Editor's Name _Jessica_

Client's Name _Matt_   Project Title _Like Father, Like Son_

Editor's Comments: Paragraph edit ~ some were too long
Great Paper Idea!

****

Client's Name _Josie_   Project Title _Dance_

Editor's Comments: Sound edit ~ only a few awkward
places. Interesting essay about a dancer's life.

****

Client's Name _Andre_   Project Title _My Mother_

Editor's Comments: Grammatical stuff — a lot of
misplaced commas and run-on sentences.

****

Client's Name _Bobby_   Project Title _My Brother Mark_

Editor's Comments: Idea edit — Just helped him
develop a few more details

****

Client's Name _Melissa_   Project Title _Beyond Hope_

Editor's Comments: Final edit — best paper I've
read all year long!

Figure 5–2. Editor's Sheet

The
Writing
Center

Media Center
or
Room 109

open
7:30 AM until 3 PM

"Beginning to Write"

To know how to begin to write is
a great art. Convince yourself
that you are working in clay, not
marble; on paper, not eternal
bronze; let the first sentence be as
stupid as it wishes. No one will
rush out and print it as it stands.
Just put it down; and then
another. Your whole first
paragraph or first page may have
to be guillotined after your piece
is finished; but there can be
no second paragraph
until you have a first.

JACQUES BARZUN

We're here to help!

Figure 5–3. Writing Center Bookmark

who would enjoy working as student editors in the Writing Center. I'm wondering whether this would be of interest to you?

Briefly, editors work as volunteers in the Writing Center or in my room (109) during study halls. These folks meet with fellow writers—students, faculty & staff, and community members—to offer assistance during all phases of the composing process. Some editors offer theme "ideas"; others work on the overall format of the piece; still others look closely at paragraph and sentence development. Frequently, the Writing Center editors are used for grammatical/technical edits.

One thing. Editors are not expected to be "super human" or perfect. Each student does the best s/he can. One thing we don't do is write the paper (story, poem, or essay) for the student. We also don't take the blame if students don't get the grade they believe they deserve. All final decisions about a paper are the writer's. Period.

What's the pay off, you ask? Good question. First, the experience. The more you edit fellow writers' work, the better writer you become. That's pretty obvious, I'm sure. Writing is a powerful way to learn.

Next, you get paid $25,000 a year . . . yes, Wendy, I'm joking.

Next, your name is listed in one of my sophomore classes. So, if you edit for the Center and keep a log of those edits, you receive extra credit (1–4 points on your quarter grade depending on the amount of editing) toward your English grade. Also, we ask that editors read and write during the summer; this beefs up your portfolio for first quarter. See the enclosed letters that I have already sent to next year's editors for further information.

And finally, virtually every college and university in the United States has a writing center or a learning center that staffs student editors. For a number of my former student colleagues who worked in the MVHS center, this experience has gotten them a job! But more, college admissions people are impressed with the fact that a student volunteered to work with other students in such a learning situation. The Writing Center is a unique idea for the high school level.

So, did I sell it? If you have questions, talk with folks like Lincoln MacIsaac, Sydney Rowe, Mike Arbor, Donna Irish or others who have volunteered in past years.

Feel free to call or write me if you have any questions. Thank you for considering this position.

Hope you're having a restful summer filled with barbecue

pig-outs, beach frolics, Coos Canyon escapes, OOB rendezvous, and a bit of reading and writing!

> Warmly, your "soon-to-be" loving English teacher,
> Richard Kent

Wendy joined the Writing Center staff that next year as a sophomore. She did an exemplary job with her fellow writers. Her plans are to join the Writing Center class her senior year.

Summer Work for Editors

Each summer kids like Wendy who plan on working in the Center write me weekly letters or keep journals. Others choose to work writing novels, short stories, essays, or poems. Another dozen or so students who won't be editors but will take English 109 opt to gain credit for the coming year by reading and writing during the summer months.

During summer break, I send eight general letters and write each student a personal response to one of their writings. Often, my personal response is a postcard.

Of the hundreds of letters I have received over the past six summers, Jamie's remains a part of me to this day.

> Mr. Kent,
>
> Something happened yesterday that changed my life. It all started when I stopped at "Bob's Kwik Stop" for a soda. I pulled in, left my car running, and hopped out. A good-neighboring friend was mowing his lawn. When I gave him a wave to say hi, he collapsed. I ran as fast as I could to him. He was having a heart attack, but I did not know this since so many things were happening so fast. I screamed for help as loud as I could, but there was no one there.
>
> Finally someone came out of the store. I yelled at them to go back into the store and call an ambulance. While that was going on I checked his pulse—he had one; a weak one, then it stopped. I then started CPR on his chest. I did not give him mouth to mouth because he was kind of choking, that means air is escaping. I stopped CPR, checked his pulse. It was slight, then it stopped again. I started pounding on his chest again. This is the scary part, I knew he was gone when his eyes bulged and his face turned purple. I watched a man die in my hands.

I know I did all I could do, but it still scares the hell out of me. The ambulance arrived, they worked on him for a half-hour there, giving him shock treatment and continued CPR. They packed him into the ambulance and took him to the hospital. I called my mother—she was working at the hospital. She said that he didn't make it. Although I knew he didn't make it when I was working on him I thought there was a chance at the hospital to revive him. It was just all too scary. All the courses I have taken on CPR etc. don't really teach you until you experience it. I am still shaking on the inside. I am going to his wake tonight since he was a friend.

I work at Thibault's Funeral Home and I deal with the dead all the time and it doesn't bother me. Seeing this living being lose life is beyond anything I can write or say. It scares me to imagine how fast life comes and goes. I just pray to God that I have a fulfilling life and that he takes me at the right time.

Sincerely,
Jamie P.

This connecting during the summer is a valuable part of my Writing Center classes. Not only do we begin building our classroom society by sharing, but I am able to isolate the basic strengths and weaknesses of my students' writing. And in a case like Jamie's, we share life moments.

Writing an Analysis

When you're sixteen years old, and it's mid-February, and you've written thirteen papers, one hundred-plus journal entries, thirty or forty pages of written book projects, and a slew of letters and reflections for your English class, subjects simply seem to disappear. I understand. These are, after all, young writers.

Many times, I will suggest they read a fellow 109er's paper and write an analysis or reaction to it. Through this exchange my young writers think and act as editors, critics, and teachers. Most students are quite serious about analyzing a peer's work.

This year, after reading Matt's poem "An Evening of Immense Nothing" in our Dead Poets' Society (DPS) chapbook, Anthony wrote an analysis of it. In this particular case, I did not suggest this topic. Anthony responded because he enjoyed the poem and because he is one of Mountain Valley's peer counselors. His final paper threaded the poem with basic research on teen alcohol abuse.

Once I read Anthony's essay, I suggested he show the piece to Matt. Interestingly, Matt responded with a letter. I did not suggest to Matt that he write in return. He felt moved to do so, saying, "I want you to know that you have created a special paper . . . I am honored."

These writings—back and forth—create a rich, authentic dialogue. They show the promise of a writing workshop in a portfolio classroom. Eventually, as Matt has illustrated, students automatically write to and about one another without my assigning it. This frequently happens when students edit one another's papers. Often, at the end of a draft, I'll find a one- or two-paragraph note to the writer. This is one more indicator that our writers' workshop is in full swing, and I am both facilitator and coach.

The next level of analysis has my students writing about one of their own pieces from earlier in the year. Some students select a paper from the year before. Most young writers, like April, find this quite illuminating:

> Last year, I thought that my paper "Rumford, The Most Boring Town in the World" was the best thing I had ever written. Boy, was I wrong. I didn't give any specifics at all. I just complained all the way through. As you would say, Mr. Kent, "It's not balanced." Here are the things that I would add now . . .

April, like many emerging writers and thinkers, made the gigantic leap to self-analysis. This happens when a young writer has a great deal of experience editing other people's work. It also occurs when students have gained a certain level of confidence in themselves.

The Assignment: Full Contact Poetry

From across the room I could see Scott's face darkening. Then, through gritted teeth, a whisper: "This is bullshit."

That early morning in April, the room stilled. Heads turned. Scott's enraged words resounded in a ripple of whispers from the lips of his classmates. For an instant, I thought he was going to shove his desk aside and get in my face. Had I not known him so well—we had worked together for six years as coach and athlete—I might have asked him to leave.

His anger was the stuff of a football captain whose team's lackluster performance had them trailing at halftime. But this was not the midpoint of a high school football match. No one was behind and no one would lose. This was poetry and Scott could not find the words.

As a teacher poet, I want my students to capture the power of poetry when they write. I believe that "power" comes from honesty and the hard work of multiple drafts. Too many of us as students have been given the assignment of writing a poem in an evening. This kind of assignment sends the wrong message. It minimizes the process and insults working poets. I can't and won't allow it.

In Room 109, poetry is a full contact sport. We live it hard, work at it seriously, and feel it deeply. Each year for six to eight weeks, 109ers breathe poetry. We study Yeats and Stevens, Robinson and Frost, Plath and cummings. We analyze, discuss, and read aloud. I want my students to learn the pleasure of reading and listening to poems, so we practice a great deal and attend readings whenever possible.

I nurture multiple interpretations, always stressing that the text reveals one meaning and our experiences reveal another. Truly, this approach demystifies poetry, making it more accessible to my students. In our discussions there is never a "No, that's not right." We are always discovering "an interesting perspective" or are asking, "How and why does the text make you feel that way?" In truth, we play with meanings.

Britton (1982) concurs: "In the last analysis, a poem is a pattern, not of sounds or of movements, but of experience: it is *an* experience, a carefully organized, structured experience. To have the experience, the reader must build his own chain of responses and no one else can do it for him, however much they explain, question, discuss" (12).

After we have read and discussed a number of poems, I ask my students to choose a poet to study. They come to know the writer by reading a biography and a selection of poems. From this work the students write either an analysis of a particular poem (I give them a model I have written) or a biographical piece.

And then . . . almost every new student in 109 has heard about *the assignment*. The thing is, they can not feel what is about to happen.

"Here's your assignment. I'm the editor of the Dead Poets' Society literary journal and your goal is to get published. I either accept or reject your poem. There are no grades. Just yes or no. You have the next six weeks to get accepted," I explain. "Even if you don't get accepted for publication, the drafts of your poem will count toward your portfolio, so keep all of them. And one more thing: I am your personal editor for each and every draft of this poem."

Six weeks? One little poem? And you're going to edit? A scattering of smiles.

Here are four of the sixteen drafts of "Going for a Ride," a mountain biking poem by tenth-grader Rob Gaudette (See Figures 5–4 to 5–7). His first attempt focused on "Satanism." Rob loves to mountain bike and he's a standout on the football team. *Why Satanism?*

"I thought it was cool," he explained.

"What do you know about Satanism?" I asked.

"Nothing really."

"Don't you think you should write about something you know? Something you care about?"

"I love to mountain bike."

"There you go."

Rob sensed he'd made it when he corrected the spelling of "adrenaline" in the fifteenth draft and presented number sixteen. When he returned for the poem later on in the day—I always do a new read of the entire poem and write comments in private—we exchanged high fives as if he had scored the winning touchdown.

Acceptance sends these young poets running into the corridors, waving their poems. Some kids have them framed; others sit quietly with a friend on the corner couch in my room reminiscing the weeks of agony. Some call their parents from the lobby phone. Truly, it is time of celebration.

Some purists would argue that my method of teaching poetry writing violates student voice and homogenizes 109 poems. Some would say that as a teacher editor I am too involved in their work, and in the end, the poem is as much mine as theirs. I understand why they would feel this way. However, I won't change because I have experienced both sides.

As for Scott, he too finally found *those* words. "Football" made it into the *1991 DPS* journal. His poem has inspired many other athletes to write.

FOOTBALL

Floating,
Hard motion.
Bronzed images of old.
A man. A ball.
Explosions of power
Like T.N.T.
Dancing, forgiving.
Coursing moves.

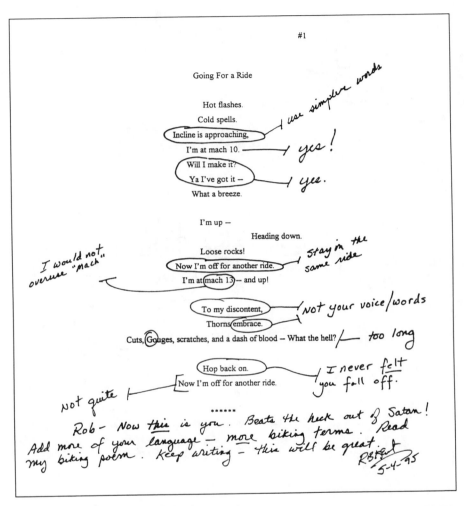

Figure 5–4. "Going for a Ride" Draft 1

Expecting.
Destinies collide
and live to rise again.
Not for glory
for love.

Scott Marchildon

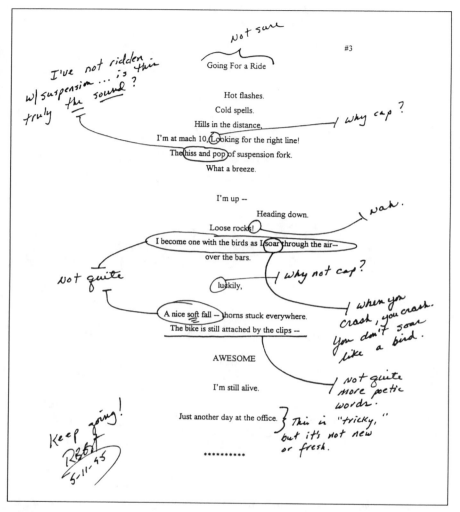

Figure 5–5. "Going for a Ride" Draft 3

Looking back at Rob's drafts and my comments, it's clear there's more to this assignment than the patience of drafting and the pain of creation. Through the various edits, students learn about using punctuation correctly. We talk about "hard" and "soft" marks of punctuation like periods and commas; we discuss the pauses they create in a poem. Most students learn that clichés don't usually work

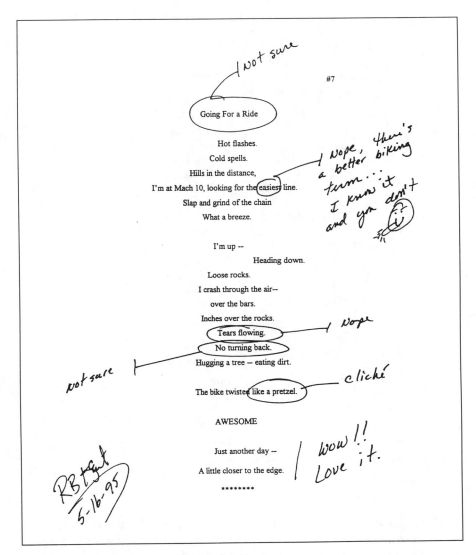

Figure 5–6. "Going for a Ride" Draft 7

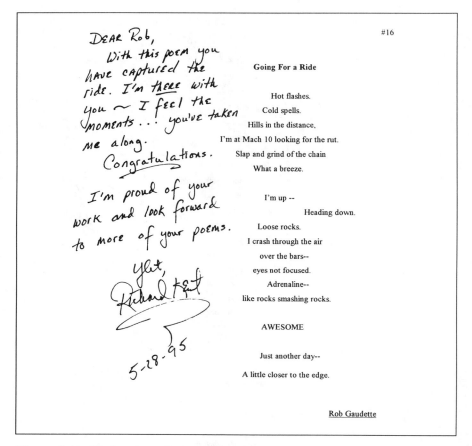

Figure 5–7. "Going for a Ride" Draft 16

well in poems or prose. One of our longest discussions revolves around metaphor. I use "Metaphors of a Magnifico" by Wallace Stevens to create what is usually a rich discussion.

At the end of the year in their reflections, my students write quite sophisticatedly *and* poetically about their experience.

> *Writing poetry seems to enlighten topics . . . It's like venturing to another world, the world of white-lined ballrooms, where I can dance to my own music. I feel as if I have taught myself a better sense of words. I can hear it in my talking and thinking, and see it in my writing. It creates a place for me*

that I can journey to anytime I want. I am always thinking up little lines that
may sometime develop into something new.

Dustin, a first-year
student

Student Poems

A few times per year we publish a chapbook of poetry. Presently, for
budget reasons, we print the books in-house. Thanks to the kids who
know how to use different desktop publishing programs as well as
the artists who supply cover art, the DPS chapbook is a fairly handsome publication. Here are a few selections:

Edge

I am alone
In the midst of
Empty faces.
Empty thoughts of
No importance.
Cold blood
Flows slowly,
Smoothly,
So unlike turmoil.
I fall apart,
Question all
Believe none.
See nothing,
Feel nothing
Rage . . . pain . . .

Janet Hoyle

An Evening of Immense Nothing

We sit in circles, laughter rolls.
I lift my glass.

Music sounds, people scream, the air cramps.
I lift my glass.

A girl falls, her beer spills.
Everyone looks, nobody moves.
I lift my glass.

A boy speaks irrelevance, another does the same.
Egos meet. A left is thrown.
I lift my glass.

Glances, again and again.
They head for the bedroom.
I lift my glass.

Same voices, same faces, different places.
I lift my glass.

Time moves, smoke spills from cigarettes.
We're all here: the druggies and the brains,
The losers and the winners.
Tonight, we're all the same.

Together, for an evening of immense nothing.
Always wondering why.
Eventually, again, I lift my glass.

Matthew Peterson

Icepick

Submerged, somewhere inside
the vent opens,
a frigid mist
encases all sensation,
molding the inexistence
of my soul.
As blessed chatter
tumbles over my lips,
I perceive the vacancy
yet continue relating words
that now contain no meaning.
A struggle ensues within,
yearning to wipe
the smile from my face,
forcing the vent to close,
I venture into new territory,
compelling my feelings to thaw.

Heidi Bonney

Double Period Exam

The crowd stands and cheers
as their boys hit the field

The players shuffle slowly
into their positions.

There is a nervous air during pre-game
filled with shouts and screams over

The sounds of rustling papers
And the grinding hum of the pencil sharpener

The siren blares, signaling
The start of the game

"This will be a double period exam."

Are you nervous?
Did you study?
Do you know all your plays?

Down-Ready-Hike-Set-Go
what's it on?

Density-Equals-Weight-Over-Volume
what's it on?

The clock ticks down
Throw the ball!
The buzzer sounds

game over . . . pencils down

Why didn't you go for it?
Why didn't you pass?

Mike Gawtry

Admission

Tears dropped
One one one
Hail, picky hail.
Black eyes
Artificial
This time true.

Porcelain mask
Shattered
Her round curves
Shook.
She no longer yearned
For the approval of men
But, the sweet, accepting love of
A woman.

Donna Irish

The Wall

I can hear the echo
of my grinding teeth
every time your closed mind
opens its mouth.
If I could breathe fire,
you'd be an inferno by now.
The harsh words I speak
still go unheard.
I struggle with the wall
you've placed in front of me,
waiting,
for just one piece to crumble.
On the quest for my future

I stand alone
for the first time.

Amy Briggs

Dead Poets' Society

A few nights a year and always the day after Thanksgiving, students
join me for a Dead Poets' Society meeting at my cabin on the shores
of Lake Webb or at my home in Rumford. The mixture of kids that
attend is fascinating, albeit unlikely. My neighbor, Don Hebert, a re-
tired business teacher at Mountain Valley, stopped two football players one Saturday evening as they strode toward my driveway, weaving
through a line of cars.

"What's going on?" he asked curious at the hubbub.

"We got a poetry reading at Kent's," shrugged Joe, an all-state football player and state champion trackster who struggled with schoolwork.

Don looked hard at the boy waiting for him to crack a smile. "What do you mean?"

"Poetry. We're having a poetry reading," said Joe holding up a poetry book as he headed up my driveway.

At our DPS meetings jocks and academics, theater kids and *the invisible* share the power of language and the songs created by the melding of words. Meetings last a couple of hours. Past and present student members gather; most read poems they have written or admired. We

---

DPS

The Dead Poets' Society
requests the honor of your presence

An opportunity to reacquaint with
old friends and to talk about life,
college, work and beyond . . .

Thanksgiving Weekend 1995
Friday the 24th
6 to 8ish in the evening
Kent's on Prospect

Casual dress (naturally),
bring a dessert (only if you'd like and
only if you can cook better than Kent),
and perhaps we'll do a reading???

Figure 5–8. Invitation to Dead Poets' Society Meeting

eat junk food and slug down liters of Maine's own Moxie while listening to offerings.

Some members work hard before our meetings to find poems that
will grab their friends around the neck or massage their hearts. Others flip through a poetry book hastily grabbed from my kitchen table
and read anything that catches their eye. Some selections are vulgar.
Others are moving. Each brings us to feel the power of words . . . this
language of life.

The Poetry Garden

In the woods next to our school, senior Lynn Lizotte, technology
teacher Phil Merrill, and volunteer students erected a series of podi-
ums through the woods, each with a different poem covered in Plex-
iglas. This was Lynn's independent study project for Room 109
during the last quarter of her senior year. In the fall and spring, students wander through *The Poetry Garden*, writing journals, creating
poems, or thinking thoughts. It's a peaceful place replete with a
small waterfall.

If I were a city teacher, I would probably create a poetry garden
along the city streets. Whatever it takes to get my young writers published and read.

Poetry Passes

With forty-something staff members writing five to ten hall passes a
day, up to four hundred poems catch the eyes of our students and
staff each and every day. The poem in Figure 5–9 is written by Mountain Valley sophomore Michael Arbor.

Writing with and for My Students

It's no secret that if one is to teach writing, one must write. This doesn't
mean an English teacher has to crank out novels or chapbooks of poetry for publication, but it does mean participating in our own writing workshops. Writing with and for my students builds the
collegiality and the community of Room 109.

Over the years I have written many poems in celebration of my students, athletes, and colleagues. Life moments move me to respond
with the poetic.

Jon captained our team to the league championship in 1989. A

Dreams

I fly.
I am the king of my domain.
I wonder with Aristotle,
discuss world affairs with Ghandi.
I compose music with Bach and
break bread with Jesus Christ.
Tuesdays, I eat lunch with the Pope.
Boundless,
I walk in the clouds and
have picnics on deserted islands.
I stand among the trees
but manage to confer with the flowers.

Michael Arbor

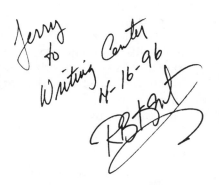

Figure 5–9. "Dreams"

few short months later, after a midday car accident, he lay in a coma. During his hospital stay, his teammates and I sat by his side talking about our matches and times together, trying as best we could to bring him home. On his birthday, I wrote this poem for Jon about his most powerful soccer game. I brought it to the hospital and gave it to his folks, my friends Brenda and Joe. Jon Sassi's battle ended seventy-seven days after the accident.

Jon's Day

That day
You could do no wrong.
That day
Powerful and confident
You ruled the pitch,
Caused opponents to stare,
Brought us all to our feet.
That day, with a silent September sky
And a whisper of feathered clouds,
You played yourself a game
And made a little magic . . .
Flick-ons, skying headers, and
Brave brilliant moves—

You played sweet string music
As you loved the moments hard.
That day—
Seven–nil
Scott for a trick
Matt with a garbage two
Dan and Mike each with one.
You never once found the net,
But, as always,
You touched us all.

RK

Each year at Mountain Valley High School we celebrate sport and friendship in Jon's memory. Hundreds of students, staff, and community people join together on a Saturday evening to play in Jon's Tournament. Faculty and staff play against a student team. Field hockey plays the girls' soccer squad; the varsity football team plays the soccer team in madcap blend of soccer and football. Alumni return; people laugh, share, and reminisce. Jon's Tournament is community at its best.

6

Beyond Writing: Reading and Projects

Self-Selected Reading

When I read a book and know that I am not going to be tested over it, I actually read it. I don't go through and look for things that may be on a test.

Kelly, a junior

During the nine-week second quarter in English 3/4 Blue last year—a heterogeneously grouped class of sophomores, juniors, and seniors—my twenty-four students collectively read 129 books. Eighty-three of those books were different titles. About thirty of the books I'd never heard of until we chatted about their selection. About fifty I had heard of but had never read. *How do you know they actually read the books?*

In Room 109, mentoring, modeling, and befriending share equal ground with reading, writing, and thinking. Again, learning is about establishing relationships. My goal is to create a "learning family" during the year. And like many families, we talk, we share, we laugh, and we argue.

I read more books this quarter than I have in my life. I hated every single one of them . . . Reading sucks! I don't even like to look at books let alone read the things!

Jonathan, a sophomore

We have an agreement in 109. My students choose their own books; and if they don't like one after reading for a while, they dump it. I refuse to treat reading as if it's some kind of medicine. You don't take it *three times a day* because it will make you better. Reading is a privilege to savor and to grow with. Reading's a way to learn and to discover. Reading helps us dream and laugh, wonder and weep.

Most of us don't become lifelong readers because we received an A on a book report. Indeed, we read because we're members of the human race looking into and beyond our own lives. We become lifelong readers by being impassioned by stories and befriending characters.

> *You know it's a good book when you get done reading it and you've learned something about yourself.*
>
> Emily, a junior

So how do I know they "actually" read a certain book? I am continually talking with my students about their reading, and they have time in class to read. They know I'm on their side. Heck, I'm like a reading cheerleader. "Mr. Kent! I read my first hardcover book!" Adam shouts from his locker down the hallway.

They're not punished or marked down because they're not readers. I begin where they are and move on from there.

Once or twice a year, we will read a book together as a class. Usually, it's *Macbeth* or *Hamlet* because sections of these plays are an absolute riot to act out in class. Plus, I love to bring Shakespeare to life with teenagers who, like me back in high school, roll their eyes at the mere mention of dear old Will.

Another aspect of self-selected reading is how students come to read certain books. I do a great deal of recommending. In addition, students learn about an interesting book during a fellow student's book project presentation or by conversations on the corner couch. "What are you reading? Is it any good?" Further, on our school district's computer network, 109 now has its own conference site called "Books 109." There, students write blurbs about books they've read recently. Truly, 109 is a readers' workshop where readers continually talk with other readers about their latest find.

My budget for books from the school department has averaged around $390 per year over the past seven years. About three dollars per kid. Yet, my classroom is filled with books. I buy books regularly and loan them out. I award extra credit for kids who visit bookstores and buy used books to donate to 109. At our local bookstores and at the public library, used books can be purchased for next to nothing, typically ten cents to a dollar. I solicit books from parents, and though I have yet to do it, I'm going to place an ad in the local paper begging for books from town folks.

In my second year of public high school teaching, I surveyed my sixty-three juniors. The results? Thirty percent of the girls considered themselves "nonreaders"—or in their words, the last thing they'd ever do would be to pick up a book to read in their free time. As for the boys, eighty percent couldn't remember having read an entire book. Was I shocked? Unh-unh. I never read an entire book in high school either. I don't think I even read an entire short story. The thing is, I didn't have to read for good grades. I took notes while listening to the teacher talk; I responded to generic questions with generic answers; I received honors grades. I did pretty much the same as an undergraduate.

What was the message I received about reading? The same one the kids in this junior class had received. First, you can get by without reading. Second, if you can get by without reading, it must not be that important.

Coaching Lisa

During her sophomore year, Lisa played a mean game of basketball and loved sports books. Her growth as a reader in 109 has been fairly typical.

Helping readers like Lisa, who are entrenched in a certain type of book, discover different books is a fun part of my job. Indeed, it is a balancing act.

To understand the impact of their reading experiences in class, I listen to what my students write in their year-end reflections. Their words reinforce my belief that each reader in class needs to be treated individually most of the time. Lisa's words speak clearly.

In the beginning of the school year I was told that I would have to read five books per quarter. I looked at Mr. Kent and smiled. But at the same time I was thinking "Are you crazy?" I might read five books per year, not once in my life have I had to read that many books in the period of nine weeks. There was no way I could finish five books.

What made this journey even worse was that I had to read five different books. If I was going to read five books they absolutely had to be over a sports related topic. My plan worked for the first quarter, but then Mr. Kent suggested different books. I tried one more time to get away with my scheme, but finally Mr. Kent sat me down and said, "You have to read a variety of books, no more basketball books!"

Of the nineteen books Lisa read, fifteen were nonsports books. In her final reflection of the year, she also admitted that her favorite book was Elie Wiesel's *Night.* I considered this a breakthrough in light of her love of sports books.

My role in this reading workshop is to chat frequently with my students and to suggest a variety of books. This is where the "balancing act" comes in. With Lisa, at the beginning of the year I let her read what she needed to read because she said five books seemed like a lot. However, after ten weeks or so, I realized she was the kind of reader who could be nudged toward different books. She responded wonderfully.

There's no denying it, a heterogeneously grouped public school language arts class is a place of difference. Some kids don't read, some kids love to read. Some kids are ready to move away from their favorite kinds of books while others simply refuse. I try my best not to force anything down their throats. Reading development, like writing, is a process. This process is enhanced through ongoing, personal conversation. That's my role as a coach of reading.

The School's Curriculum

At the present moment, our curriculum focuses on the following as a guide for reading at various grade levels in language arts:

9th grade: Genre (short stories, novels, poetry, essay, etc.)

10th grade: Multicultural with an emphasis on World Literature

11th grade: American Literature

12th grade: Multicultural with an emphasis on British Literature

We have no set number of books that students are required to read in a year on any level. As a rule, students in 109 are supposed to read at least five books of their twenty from the grade-level requirements above. There are times when nonreaders or reluctant readers do not fulfill this requirement. Yes, they still pass the class.

In every way possible, students are treated as individuals.

English ain't English anymore.

Vance, a first-year student

Projects

Drawings, maps, notes, artifacts. Interviews. Tia's illustrated "dream journal." Richard's gingerbread man cookies to snack on while we listen to his talk on Piers Paul Read's *Alive*. Andrea's AIDS quilt for Susan and Daniel Cohen's *When Someone You Know Is Gay*. Jason's Picassoesque painting of Thoreau's cabin.

Photographs, dioramas, a miniature gallows, a full-scale pillory, and stories, always stories. In one class we learn to disco dance; in another it's fly tying. Sarah presents on abuse; Jamie wraps himself in chains for his talk. Sydney bakes a cake. Mark and Corey sing an original song. With candles and an African bag, Donna eloquently shares her impressions of Sarah Lawrence Lightfoot's *Balm in Gilead*.

During our discussions on *difference*, students invite members of Maine's Gay/Lesbian Alliance to join us. In another class, we chat with award-winning sports writer Bob McPhee. Since a high school football accident in the 1970s, Bob has lived with quadriplegia and communicates with a Liberator (a computer that speaks). He's an inspiration and role model for all of us here in the valley. Bob's also a prince of a guy who, as we say in Maine, has a *wicked* sense of humor.

The auditorium is still and dark as Ryan, who has recently finished reading Art Spiegelman's *Maus I*, leads his blindfolded classmates in. Hands on shoulders, they scuff down the long aisle.

Suddenly, screams echo from the large speakers above. Students chuckle a bit.

"SHUT UP!" bellows Ryan. "MARCH!"

Silence. A few more steps, and they catch the scent.

A girl groans.

"SILENCE! YOU WILL BE SHOT!"

The screams grow louder as the chain of students tiptoe up the wooden staircase onto the stage. Ryan shoves each student onto the floor. The putrid smell is overwhelming.

"TAKE OFF YOUR BLINDFOLDS!"

On the dimly lit stage they face an immense Nazi flag, Cimmerian red with a black swastika emblazoned in the center. The large television screen flicks on. *Night and Fog* (Real Images). The steady drone of a monotone voice. Piles of skeletonized bodies. The gas chambers. Children. Women. Men. People.

The burning hair in the corner of the stage smolders.

For a moment, we feel . . .

Figure 6–1. Drawing from Tia's Dream Journal

Figure 6–2. Drawing from Tia's Dream Journal

With Chopin playing in the background, Sandra reads her poem in celebration of Dawna Lisa Buchanan's *The Falcon's Wing*. In their final reflections for the year, many of Sandra's classmates call her project the most outstanding of the year.

Darcy's oil painting over Franz Kafka's *Metamorphosis* draws a crowd when displayed on my classroom door. I purchased the painting, with dark brooding colors, the day after she presented it.

They remove tiles from the ceiling of Room 109. Secure the ropes. A rescue.
"On belay," cries Joshua, hands chalked.
"Climb!" calls Aaron.
Across the dirty yellow wall, traversing the metal bookcases.
We're on the face of a rock 800 feet up.

The clippers come out.
Victor and Richard planned it. Brian joined in at the last moment. My novel *The Mosquito Test* prompted it.
Victor explains, "When Kevin shaved his head for Scott (a character who had lost his hair to chemotherapy), I was proud of him. I needed to do something like that. I wanted to give something up."

Sunday morning. Nine o'clock. Lincoln, Jarod, and Eric trudge up the side of White Cap Mountain. They wander around the three overgrown cellars of this nineteenth-century farm. Except for an occasional yawn and mumble, they say nothing. It is, after all, early. It is also May—three weeks from graduation.
After ten minutes of roaming around, Lincoln calls out. "Look at this." He points inside the smallest of cellars twenty yards off the steep gravel road. Soon, the three boys scratch at the ground and unearth parts of red clay pots and hazy blue glassware.
"This glass is melted. Look."
"Think this building might have burnt down?"
"I wonder if this is where they stored their food?"
"I think so, guy. The big one was the barn. That one must have been the house. This is like a storage shed."
They dig deeper and in a wider area. Their speech quickens. Voices grow animated. They spread the booty out on a plastic sheet. Eric sketches the cellar where they found the pieces. Lincoln writes notes in his field journal. Jarod keeps digging.

"Look!" shouts Jarod. He uncovers the rusted blade of a scythe and lifts it for his friends to see.

"This is great," says Lincoln. "This is awesome."

His voice trails off as I stride down the mountain road. Together, they'll keep digging up yesterday. Together, without their teacher, they'll keep discovering and learning.

"I don't know what to do for a project."

"Look around the room for some ideas," I suggest.

"There's too many. Just give me one to do, Mr. Kent."

I smile. "Sorry."

Activity. People working and trying out. Some of the projects end up miserably. Students discuss the weaknesses with me and then again in their quarter-end reflections. We learn by doing, yet not everything we do is successful. Other projects are beyond our wildest dreams. In either case learning happens from that not-so-new teacher called experience.

Project Masters

I am experimenting these days by having a student keep track of projects for the quarter. The student's role as a project master is to encourage colleagues to give a presentation every two weeks and to keep track of those presentations on a master list. This helps all of us in 109 stay organized.

Writing About Reading

One of the ways I guide my student colleagues in their responses to literature is through a class letter. Here's an example focused on books. Of their three to five book projects, at least one must be written.

My Dear Students,

Yesterday, with all the good intentions in the world, I drove to Rangeley with Little Ralph, my notebook computer. My plan? To write to you about self and nature, life and books . . . you know, *stuff*.

But, I ate too many bagels and slugged down ginger ale like it was my last meal. The result? I didn't do the letter.

So, this sunny Monday morning a hasty letter about your written book project. Here are a few suggestions. You may write about these, or

Project Master List

1	Ellen	Shoe Box	t-shirt	Barn		
2	Jeffrey	Pictures	....	....	....	....
3	Michael	song	Buddha			
4	Lindy	Circus Tent	shoe	poster		
5	Sandra	diarama	model/book	Model	model	
6	Jason	Poster	cross			
7	Andie	Time Line				
8	Dan	Sled	poster	basketball		
9	Dawn	Pepsi Bottle	Village			
10	Serene	Daisy thing	trees/posters	model		
11	David	religion display				
12	Tim	Morrison Pic	Big Clock	t-shirt		
13	Katie	poster	poster			
14	Samantha	Model	Van			
15	Ryan	Court Room				
16	Rene	Painting				
17	Kerrie	Poster	Poster			
18	Jessica	Bus				
19	Darcy	Model	Blanket			
20	Lauralee	MA Diarama	book display	poster		
21	Troy	model				
22	Chad	Hitler's Head	voodoo doll			
23	Adam	song				

Figure 6–3. Project Master List

you may write about anything you come up with on your own. **This is a guide.** The bottom line is, however, that you write for a few hours about your book. Use first draft, freewrite and spellcheck, please.

Enjoy. (*I know, I know . . .*)

Coming to Know Your Reading
Through Reflection

"A Book Project for 109"

(Remember: these questions are a guide.
You may use some, or none, or come up with your own focus.)

1. In a paragraph or two, tell the plot (what happens) of this book.

2. Why should someone read this particular book? What lessons can we learn by reading and thinking about this book?

3. What character do you most relate to in your book? Why? Would she or he be a friend of yours? What characteristics of this person do you admire? What makes this person stand out above others in this book?

4. What character bothers you the most in this book? Why? Would this be one of those people you'd most likely get into a fight with? Are they simply annoying? Dishonest? Sappy? A goody-two-shoes (or is that a goody-too-shoes)?

5. If you liked this book, what three factors made you like it? List them and explain them. What other good books have you read that had similar "good points"?

6. If you weren't all that partial to the book, why is that? Why did you finish it? Even though you didn't exactly like it, what was the good stuff of the book?

7. How did you happen to pick this book out of ALL the books available? Did someone recommend it to you? If so, why did you take their recommendation?

8. In the great scheme of things, why is this book a piece that everyone should read? If it not one of *those* books, why not?

9. How did the setting (where the book took place) affect the characters? How was the setting important to the book?

10. Assuming the author is still alive, write a letter to her or him in a few short paragraphs explaining how this book was important to you. (This should be mailed to the author in care of the publisher. Look at the inside cover for address information.)

11. Write a letter to your younger sister or cousin or friend that explains the value of this book. Convince them that they should read it.

12. What was the power scene of the book? Explain this.

13. What part of the book could have been left out and why?

14. Did the author do a good job of writing the dialogue? How so?

15. Even if you disliked the book, could you see why some people would enjoy it? Who are those people and why would they enjoy the book?

16. Talk about the various secondary characters in the book. How are they important to the book and to the main characters?

17. If you know anything about the author, what parts of the book reflect her or him? For example, if you read my book you'd see a lot of stuff about high schools. I know high schools pretty well. So, talk about the author's "knowing" and the book itself.

18. If this was a book you couldn't put down, what other books similar to it have you read? What makes them this good? Further, what turns you on to a book?

19. Assuming you liked your book, what would you say if someone said, "That book was the worst book I have ever read"?

20. How did this book create balance in your life? What did this book do for your "self"?

21. How was the main character balanced or unbalanced? What created balance for her or him?

22. Remember when we talked about *point of view*? What did the "point of view" have to do with your liking or disliking the book?

Enough. As you can see, I could keep listing questions until the proverbial cows come home. This is a good start, however. Come up with your own questions, if you'd like. Read and rely on these totally. Whatever does it for you. Enjoy. Think. Write. Reflect. Do.

Always, YLET,
Rich Kent

I have discovered two books that have extended my understanding and my thinking about reader-centered classrooms. Janet Allen's *It's Never Too Late: Leading Adolescents to Lifelong Literacy* is especially helpful when considering "at risk" students. Jeffrey D. Wilhelm's *"You Gotta BE the Book": Teaching Engaged and Reflective Reading with Adolescents* is a remarkable study about dramatic and artistic response to literature. Wilhelm has been invaluable as I guide my students in "outgrow(ing) themselves," not only as readers but as writers, thinkers, learners, and in a real sense, as people.

7

And Finally, the Portfolio

A 109 Portfolio: Brooke's Book

In her quarter-end English reflection, Brooke wrote, "I love to express myself by speaking." In Room 109, Brooke not only led discussions, but she listened intently and responsively. By the end of the grading period, she had also produced a well-developed, interesting portfolio. She was, in a word, a scholar. Out of school, Brooke led alpine ski racers in Maine by capturing the Class "A" slalom crown during her junior year.

Fortunately for me and her classmates in Period 3/4 Blue, Brooke chose to come back to 109 for another year in English as a member of the Writing Center class. During the summer she read five books and wrote seven letters to me. For the first quarter of her junior year, Brooke fulfilled the basic requirements of a 109 portfolio while earning extra credit for volunteering in the Writing Center two to three times per week. She also volunteered to read and respond to other students' portfolios—a practice that is now required of all my students.

It's difficult to call Brooke's first-quarter portfolio "ordinary." Yet, in some respects it is. Her book includes five papers, fifty journal entries, eight and a half books (Brooke is a reader), four projects, and the extras mentioned above. Our class themes for the quarter focused on self, nature, and balance. She touched on two of those themes—self and balance—with her writings (see Figures 7–1(a) and 7–1(b)).

Brooke's papers are engaging and diverse. She begins with a personal narrative that recounts the discoveries she made on two college visitations. Her opening paragraph of "Finding My Gold Mine" is a real grabber:

> After I hung up the phone I sat back, sighed, and thought, "I'm on my way." I had just finished a conversation with Katie Sassi, who now

---

109 Portfolio Cover Sheets

1st Quarter

Name _Brooke Carey_   Phone _369-9434_
Period _3/4 B_   Year _Junior_

Formal Papers

Title _Finding My Gold Mine_
Theme _a reflection of my visits to two colleges._
_____
How many drafts included? _6_

Title _Bad Girls_
Theme _a short story about teenage girls_
_____
How many drafts included? _6_

Title _I Believe_
Theme _a reflection on religion and what I have_
learned
How many drafts included? _5_

Informal Papers
Title _Credo_
Theme _____
_____
How many drafts included? _3_

Title _all about Me_
Theme _The autobiography I wrote in the_
beginning of the year
How many drafts included? _2_

Figure 7–1. Brook's Portfolio Cover Sheet

attends a school in Vermont. I spoke with her because I was planning to visit this school and I wanted to stay overnight to get the full effect of the college. It had been my first choice for at least two or three years. All that changed in a matter of fifty hours.

In "Bad Girls," Brooke creates a short story of a teenage athlete who becomes too involved in the party scene. In this particular piece, like so many young writers, Brooke spends a great deal of time

---

Books

List the books you've read for 109 English:

Let 'Em Eat Cake   Little Girls in Pretty Boxes

Breaking the Surface   a different kind of Christmas

The Stoning of Soraya   True Crime

Prozac Nation   Balm in Gilead (½)

Girl

How many one-page, 150-word journal entries have you written? _50_

What extras have you included in your portfolio -or- accomplished this quarter?

(e.g. portfolio reader, editor)

During the summer I wrote you seven letters and read five books. I was also an editor in the Writing Center.

Projects

Thoroughly describe and explain each project you presented to us in English this

quarter. Include your written book projects, too.

- Janel and I spent eight and one half hours scraping, painting and hanging a chairlift for the poetry garden.

- Sketched and painted a picture of Greg Louganis

- Janel and I made a cake and then decorated it for the book "LET 'EM EAT CAKE"

- Seven and one half page written book project over GIRL

Figure 7–1. Continued

"telling" the story in longish narrative paragraphs. Quick, meaning-ful dialogue is missing, a point I neglected to make in my summary letter to her.

In "I Believe," we witness the introspective Brooke as she looks closely at her religious beliefs.

That spring and summer was a struggle. Unfortunately, I was too big and too old to continue to fall asleep in church. I had no excuse. So, with no where left to go, I started to listen to the sermon. That summer I learned some things about my religion.

Like Brooke, her autobiography is fun and interesting. For three of the six pages she focuses on her relationships with her sister Briah and friend Janel. She calls them her "best friends." Then we're treated to the eclectic Brooke as she dashes from subject to subject with passion, insight, and humor.

I have noticed that I only like to spend time in my bedroom when it is clean. I find that funny considering it is hardly ever clean enough so that I can see the floor. But if I have a spare Saturday or Sunday, I usually take the morning and clean my desk and floor, and then if I am really ambitious I will even vacuum. The result is so nice. I will actually be able to breathe in my room and relax.

When I am sitting back and relaxing in my clean room, I usually read and/or listen to music. Lately I have been into astrology. It is whacked how everything is connected. I am a Virgo and it says that I can worry a cold into pneumonia and that I have to analyze everything . . . I cannot believe that the way I act is based on a few stars in the sky.

Brooke's "Credo" shines with the beliefs of a young woman with energy, caring, and intellect. Her four-page list of "what I believe in" creates a picture. Here are a few of my favorites:

Don't turn your back from a problem, solve it.

Smile and laugh often. It looks more attractive and it makes you feel good.

A little procrastination never hurt anybody.

Fake people suck.

Never eat potato chips or drink soda.

Never say "never."

Just get over it.

Mix it up.

Dig yourself.

Learn all of the rules and then break some.

Every now and then, bite off more than you can chew.

Check for toilet paper before sitting down.

The more you know the less you fear.

Diversity is beautiful.

Brooke's journal entries sing with a confident voice. As with her credo and autobiography, she cruises from subject to subject with ease. Not all of the entries are the required 150 words in length, and some read more like day-to-day diary entries than idea journals, but the overall song created is pleasant, interesting, and revealing.

Brooke's projects continue to shine with *difference*. Refurbishing and hanging a ski chairlift in our school's poetry garden with Janel has brought pleasure to those who spend quiet time reading and writing there. Brooke's painting of Greg Lougainis is colorful and precise; her cake was delicious. As I've written in my letter response, her written book project relied heavily on plot summary. A bit more playfulness is called for.

Teacher's portfolio response

Dear Brooke,

There's so much about you that is powerful and interesting. You know, as much as I dump on your *spirited* way, I do admire you and know that you're going to have a wonderful life.

I had a blast reading your essay about your trip to Katie's school. You were so perceptive in this piece. I admire the fact that you respect diversity. Perhaps the subject of diversity should be a full-blown paper? It's interesting that a young womyn from Rumford would be so tuned in to difference. Why? Why aren't other kids so sensitized? Is it your family? Your travels? Why? All of this is deeply interesting to me.

Be careful about the length of some of your paragraphs. Some tend to ramble on. A simple glance at the lengths of each paragraph in relation to another is usually a key. I know that sounds simple—it is. I like the details in your writing. You always load up your essays and stories with the *things* of life. That brings up my interest level.

Your credo is special. The many sides of you come out in this piece. If I were going to improve on this, it would be to expand your concluding paragraph to usher the reader out. Make sense? Your written book project is a bit on the plot summary side, but still interesting. Watch out for the little technical problems. You misplace commas and some sentences read awkwardly. Not horrible by any means—just not perfect. (No, I don't want you to be perfect!)

Once again your journals are diverse. I appreciated your honesty about the Lougainis book; I also admire the work you put into the chairlift w/ Janel. It's a wonderful addition to the poetry garden. Thank you! Also, nice work on the summer letters. Very solid, mature and sophisticated.

Thanks. That's it. I look forward to hearing more from you as time goes on this year. You've got a great way about you . . . when you leave me alone!

YLET,
Rich Kent

Keeper letter

Brooke's father wrote the *keeper* response to this portfolio.

Dear Reader,

I didn't start the review of Brooke's work with a very positive frame of mind. It was given to me at the last minute when the hour was late and I had much already to do. Once I settled into the review, however, I was not disappointed.

Again, unfortunately, I have had to read words to have a better understanding of who Brooke is. She is outspoken to begin with, but her writing is deeper and more honest so I naturally enjoy it very much. Of course the truth can be painful, but after all it is no more than another teenager growing up and, like most of us have done, finding our own way.

Once again I extend my gratitude to this whole process. I believe there is wisdom afoot here and I appreciate it. Thank you Rich and good job Brooke! I know you a bit better now.

Tom C.

Brooke's first-quarter portfolio offers a fine example of studious work. She went above and beyond with her books and volunteerism; her papers were revised thoroughly. She also spent a good deal of time working on English in the summer. Her final assessment for the quarter, including the extra credit, was a well-deserved high honors grade of ninety-four.

During the last quarter of her junior year, Brooke took her learning to another level by venturing off to investigate the life and poetry of Sylvia Plath. With this work, she began to show her ability to undertake independent study much like Jeremy, whose portfolio is reviewed next.

In my final portfolio letter to her at the end of the year, I wrote, "I'm proud to have been your teacher." Indeed, Brooke is a woman of great promise who makes a difference in our world.

Personalizing Portfolios

In a portfolio pedagogy no two classes are the same just as no two portfolios are ever alike.

Once students get comfortable with both the workshop atmosphere and the responsibility that goes along with that freedom, often they come to me with proposals for developing their own distinctive portfolios. The following is a preliminary plan I happened to have received today.

Hunting project

Josh D. and I, Dusty H., have decided that we want to do a project over hunting. The following is a list of ideas that we may use during the course of our study.

1. We plan to talk hunting stories and record them onto a tape. These are going to be exaggerated stories that will be comical. We will write out the stories first and pass in the drafts.

2. We plan to make a hunting video. We are thinking that we will have the film edited to some way have it look like the Top Cops show. We will write out the outline of the video. The video will include strategies (where to hunt, hunting safety tips, how to stay unseen and quiet, etc.), discussion of different caliber rifles, discussion of hunting laws, the preparation for the hunt, and the process of field dressing and skinning a deer.

3. We will cut the outline of a deer body out of cardboard. On one side we will draw the meat patterns and correct bullet placement on the other. We may try to laminate this somehow so that we may use markers during our presentation.

4. We will bring in different types of meat for people to try. We may not label the meat but rather let the students try to guess what it is. We were thinking either different types of meat from just deer (heart, liver, tenderloin, shoulder, etc.), or different types of

animal meat (deer, squirrel, moose, etc.). We could compare these meats to regular beef.

5. We will take pictures and make a portfolio. These pictures will include timed sequenced events that happen throughout a day of hunting.

6. We were thinking about interviewing people. We will ask their feelings on the topic of hunting and will write up the responses in a short paper.

7. We will try to get a scheduled ride with a game warden. We will interview him and also include this in the short paper.

8. We will read books and magazines. We will also write papers to fill the proper requirements of the class.

Other ideas may arise, and if they do we will bring them to your attention.

Before portfolios, I might have felt that Dusty and Josh were trying to finagle their way out of real English. Something inside me would have balked at the thought of kids actually wanting to do work to the point of developing their own plans.

Dusty and Josh are avid hunters. Some might consider their proposal more of a science project than an English assignment. The thing is, look at the detail of this preliminary prospectus, a plan they developed totally on their own. Each of the elements of our language arts class is included: reading, writing, listening, speaking, viewing, observing, presenting, and performing. Additionally, they plan to video, interview, photograph, apprentice, and cook. The fact that their project revolves around a theme that they're passionate about is a bonus. Plus, once we meet I might have some suggestions.

For reading, depending on what they ultimately select, I might suggest portions of Thoreau's *Walden* as well as *The Hurricane Island Book of Readings*. Another favorite of mine is *Nature I Loved* by Bill Geagan. Once we chat about their plan, I will get a better sense of the amount of writing they will do. However, they have already assured me that "we will also write papers to fill the proper requirements of the class."

What's tricky about their proposal is that their class is moving into an eight-week study with an emphasis on acting, plays, speeches, and improvisations. We call this *Stage 109*. I want these two young men to be a part of the productions. Both Dusty and Josh are a lot of fun in these situations. So, we'll negotiate. Sometimes they'll participate in class; sometimes they'll be off doing their research. If they agree to this, the project will be a go.

I'm continually consulting with students. Though, as the year progresses, they catch on and need less input from me about work levels and standards. Kristin came to me today with a proposal to write a twelve- to fifteen-page short story and count the piece as two papers for her portfolio. The same type of thing happened with Mike's stained glass window in celebration of Sam Keen's *Fire in the Belly: On Being a Man.* His dad taught him the art; ten hours later Mike completed a striking glass book cover. This was no ordinary project.

Kim spoke with me yesterday about her portfolio. All five of her papers (a short story, a credo, a narrative, two essays) were thirteen to fifteen hundred words long and each had been edited extensively. Needless to say, she'd gone above and beyond, too. Her final assessment would reflect the incredible effort she'd put forth, and now that she's gone beyond with her portfolio and personalized it, she'll probably venture even more.

Tim announced that he had finished reading his seventh book; several other students revealed they had written six or seven papers instead of five. Each of those students knows he or she has gone beyond the basic requirements. They also know the decision is in their hands.

When we focus on poetry, as you've seen in "Full Contact Poetry," the poem they compose usually counts as a formal paper because it is thoroughly revised over four to six weeks. Likewise, if we study short stories, a student's story like Kristin's twelve- to fifteen-pager might fill up part of the formal or informal paper requirement depending on its length. Ultimately, students choose whether they want to draft the piece thoroughly to make it a formal paper or only once for an informal. If they tire of a certain writing project and decide to dump it before completion, they put what they've written into their journal or into an "extra" section to receive credit for their efforts.

Along with the portfolio cover sheets that I supply, many students personalize their portfolios by writing introductory letters and a table of contents. Some, like James, produce thematic covers for each of their quarter portfolios (see Figure 7–2).

Some students come up with their own special way to keep track of their progress through the quarter. Victor's organizational chart is a fine example (see Figure 7–3).

"There is no **enemy** other than
The man who is **not open to everything**"
--Allan Bloom

Put your feet ***down***--students should *look* like they're doing work!!

"Keep on *rockin'* in the **free** world   cottleston, cottleston, cottleston pie

Why? . . . Why not?   Dress codes are great!!! yes, yes, yes!

To be, or not to be? **That** is the question.

"Four score and Seven Years ago, our fathers set forth to . . ."
--HONEST Abe Lincoln

Truth, justice, and the American way

"I have a dream" You talk, I'll pretend to listen.

"I'm not just your principal, I'm your princi***pal***"
stop that right now   *sit down and shut up*

So, you say you want a revolution?

the powers that *be*   peace is cheap, but who's buying?

Question Authority?(no) (yes)check one,please

The word 'WE' must never be placed first within man's

soul.**"Without *Rules* there is Chaos!!!"**

Without conformity, students can't learn . . . nothing
gets accomplished

*!!***POWER***!!*   *UH-Oh!*

Ah-Ha!   take it to a vote   **I.R.A.**

Power to the people. Democracy works--sort of--if you're rich.

God   ....*and for goodness sake,*

Take off that Hat!!

Figure 7-2. James's Thematic Cover Sheet

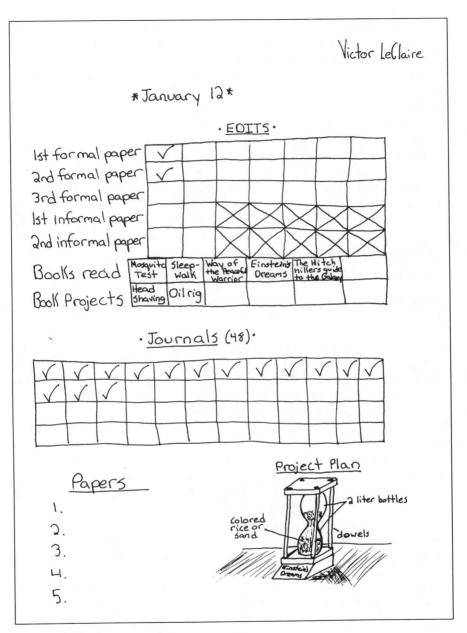

Figure 7–3. Victor's Organizational Chart

Portfolio pedagogy is responsive to individuals and to the classroom society as it actually is, not as the teacher, the curriculum, or a book on pedagogy might like it to be. This way, students and their products are the driving force behind the class. They feel in charge, and they are in charge. They feel respected, and they are respected. Do they *always* make the best decisions? Do they *always* use this power well? Do you? Do I? Does anyone?

Here's the bottom line: Young people, as a way of being initiated into the adult learning world, need an opportunity in school to make as many decisions and to wield as much power as possible in the classroom and beyond. They also must face the consequences of their actions. This is the reality of a portfolio pedagogy.

An Independent Study Portfolio: Jeremy's Investigation

I like to treat my learning like an adventure or a mission.

Jeremy, a junior

There's a stunning moment in *Horace's Compromise* when we come to know the meaning behind the title. In Sizer's (1992) sequel, *Horace's School*, we learn how Horace, a veteran English teacher, views his students: "Many are lively, well intentioned, and adept at cranking out acceptable test scores, but they are without the habits of serious thought, respectful skepticism, and curiosity about much of what lies beyond their immediate lives" (1).

Most students find portfolio classrooms *the* most freeing experience of their school careers. Jeremy is a prime example. After spending his sophomore and junior years in Room 109, Jeremy chose to return for a third year. During his first two years, he pretty much followed the standard requirements of portfolios, focusing on the basic themes we discussed. During the fourth quarter when all students are now required to pursue some independent project, Jeremy let his love of the outdoors take over.

As an eleventh grader, Jeremy designed and mapped out a hiking trail through the Longfellow Mountains here in western Maine. During this fourth-quarter independent study, "Trail 109" became a reality. Topographical maps, weekend hikes, and a variety of books drove his investigation that culminated in a presentation to his classroom colleagues.

During the first quarter of his senior year, Jeremy knew what he wanted to do for an investigation and simply got on with it. His project focused on black holes and The Big Bang Theory, a galaxy away from our work with *diversity, ethics,* and *boredom.* Yet, Jeremy took a lively role in our class discussions. At times, he was a force. But when the conversations ended and workshop time commenced, Jeremy frequently headed off to the media center to research or to work on his calculus. Jeremy enjoys writing at home on his own computer.

At the front of his portfolio, Jeremy included a three-page letter. The highlight of this letter for me consists of these three sentences:

> My independent study project was an interesting experience. It was certainly a venture out of the norm. I definitely did expand my knowledge; I would say I'm the resident expert on black holes at our school.

Expressing this kind of confidence speaks volumes about Jeremy *and* his independent study.

Jeremy's mom provided the *keeper* letter for this particular portfolio. Her description of the moments surrounding the coming of portfolio day bring us right into the Broughton household.

Reflections from Mom

The clicking of computer keyboard keys has begun to be constant over the past several weeks. The moments of silence, then click, clickety click again only means one thing at 222 Penobscot Street, that the quarter is closing down and deadlines have to be met and Jeremy's projects, papers, books, and journals are uniting together with one common goal, to be finished and in to Room 109.

The spatters of paint still remain on the counter top and kitchen floor as tell tale signs of the evening spent with a mess of black poster board, running to every automotive store to search for funnels all over town, xmas lights I had to so willingly give up so that you could create through the night an awesome project of a Black Hole.

As I read through your portfolio I can see how in depth your writings are and I begin to see how differently you see things and how well you put your thoughts on paper. I also love your comparison of mathematics to summer and winter and agree how wonderful summer time is and how rigid mathematics are, like winter.

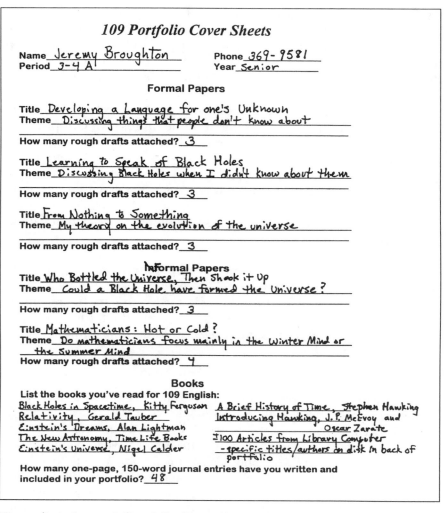

Figure 7–4. Jeremy's Portfolio Cover Sheet

You mentioned how easily you can get distracted when writing outside, with the snapping of a twig, but as you know Jeremy, our living quarters is like being in a jungle with two little monkeys and one 13 year old Orangutan, but you have done well to accomplish these pieces despite it all.

It saddens me when you say in your letter to Coach that, "Here's

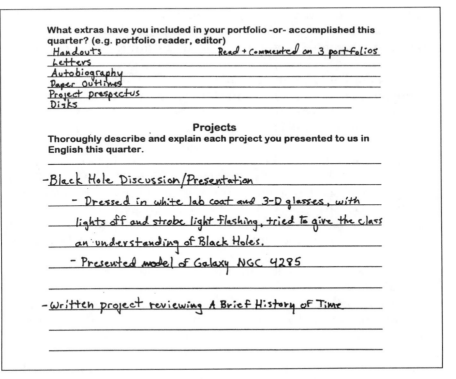

What extras have you included in your portfolio -or- accomplished this quarter? (e.g. portfolio reader, editor)

Handouts   Read + Commented on 3 portfolios
Letters
Autobiography
Paper Outlines
Project prospectus
Disks

Projects

Thoroughly describe and explain each project you presented to us in English this quarter.

-Black Hole Discussion/Presentation

    - Dressed in white lab coat and 3-D glasses, with lights off and strobe light flashing, tried to give the class an understanding of Black Holes.

    - Presented model of Galaxy NGC 4285

-written project reviewing A Brief History of Time

Figure 7–4. Continued

to this year, my last" but it is true, and you've worked hard and I know it will be the best yet for you. You have grown and developed some great writing skills thanks to these Portfolios from Room 109.

Love, Mom

P.S. Only three P's to go!

Jeremy kept an archive of his initial plans for the study. He included this in the back of his portfolio. In his notes from the eight-week investigation, scribbles and drawings, not unlike those I have kept while developing this book, appear throughout. And why not, both of us are creating. Both of us are writers and thinkers focusing forwardly and inwardly as we make meaning. This is what scholarship is about.

Reading Jeremy's notes is a study unto itself. His thinking unfolds and his ideas add layers, overlap, and gently move toward a new level of understanding. From his initial plan, replete with sketches, Jeremy's notes begin to show how he makes meaning of the concept:

> The primordial egg—how can all this mass and weight be compressed to the size of a pinhead? Quintessential law of physics—matter cannot be created or destroyed. So *everything* must have been inside of the egg. How? No language . . . can't even imagine.

From these notes, "no language" became a key for his thoughtful paper entitled "Developing a Language for One's Unknown." In this piece Jeremy discusses science and metaphor, black holes and boat propellers. His struggle with creating a language that includes concepts that are beyond human understanding—and thus beyond human language—is a model of searching. Listen to a few of his lines:

> Have you ever tried to describe something that you know very little about?
>
> Imagine an overweight person trying to describe the exhilaration a marathon runner feels when crossing the finish line. If they have never run a race before it would be difficult . . . They would have no language to describe it. However, they would be able to come close by making comparisons to similar situations in their own life . . . they would be able to describe the runner's feeling by comparing it to, say, the way they feel at the top of the stairs after they have just climbed them.
>
> In order to describe something we need to understand it ourselves, or we only describe our misunderstandings. In order to understand something we must be able to speak the subject's language. We must be able to explain it to ourselves by making comparisons and references to things in our own life. We need to make meaning of it for ourselves.
>
> As finite beings, we have a very difficult time trying to describe infinite things . . . It makes it even worse in trying to describe infinity because our language is time based . . . All of our verb tenses are based on past, present and future, none of which exist in anything infinite.

For his final presentation, Jeremy dressed in a white lab coat and wore 3-D glasses as a "science guy." With shades drawn and lights off, he lit his carefully constructed "black hole" with sparkling stars courtesy of his mom's Christmas lights. Jeremy's talk helped each of us move closer to an understanding of our universe and its workings. Indeed, Jeremy was the teacher.

Teacher's Portfolio Letter Response

Dear Jeremy,

I loved the way your mom described your house and you during portfolio crunch time. Wonderful!

You continue to impress me. Both in class and within your writing/thinking of your portfolio. Your strengths in analogy and metaphorical thinking bring your essays to another level. Your voice throughout is consistent, inviting and thoroughly readable. There are certain technical writing problems, but they don't detract terribly from the overall power of your work. Indeed, these are thoughtful.

"Language . . ." is so very interesting. I am stealing some of your comparisons! You might like to read my teacher's book on language. James Britton has produced some of the most influential writings and thinking in the world on the subject of language and learning. It is amazing stuff. Amazing. Your analogy of a toddler learning to speak—a.k.a. language acquisition—is the focus of much of James Britton's research. Another mentor, Michael Armstrong, also does much with this. I have tons of information on this and deep interest in it, so think about this as a study, too.

All of this work focuses on making meaning for yourself. It is so very powerful on one level. I wish I had more energy and more time right now to write a scholarly response. Truthfully, I could barely brush my teeth this morning! Ha. The portfolio blues. Anyway, November is a great month to sit and chat, don't you think? We should grab Peterson and anyone who'd like to experiment and explore some thoughts. What do you think?

Back to your thinking. I have a brilliant book of poetry—*Before It Vanishes* by Robert Pack—that celebrates Pagel's *Cosmic Code*. I think you should read this for the "summer mind" side of cosmology and your thinking about our universe. (I'm beginning to falter . . . You know what? I think I'm going to drool on my keyboard.)

I need a copy of your independent study and your math project. Both are intriguing to me. Both are so well synthesized. The technical stuff that is wrong just doesn't seem to interrupt my reading; yet, you should come to grips with the need for developing better skills that way. You're not horrible—it is just a bit weak here and there.

Your presentation was creative, well conceived and interesting. I'm pleased that you have the insight to bring such a level of work to your classmates. Thank you for your work this quarter. I admire you.

YLET&C,

Coach

After Jeremy presented his portfolio, he spent the next week—the time during which I read and respond to portfolios—writing his reflection of the experience. I offer certain questions as prompts, but encourage students to follow their own thinking. (Reflections are covered later on in the book.)

Jeremy's fifteen-page, four-thousand-word response helped me see his thought processes more clearly. In truth, he invited me in for an intimate, no-holds-barred look at his struggles and his successes. When students reach this level of reflection, I feel like a voyeur. I am sure this piece helped him look more closely at how he researches, thinks, writes, and learns.

Portfolios encourage young scholars to play with ideas. Surely, Jeremy's writing and thinking is playful, thoughtful, and searching. It is clear that this young man is a theorist, a scientist, a writer, and a thinker . . . a serious student. Horace would be proud.

Organizing the Laundry Baskets

When people drop by my room, especially around the infamous "Portfolio Day," their looks say it all. *Do you have a life?*

When faced with the mass of paper and three-ring binders, the whole idea of portfolio assessment can be pretty daunting. Heck, just organizing the collection of 120 student books is an undertaking. I bought plastic rectangular laundry baskets on sale at the local discount store; they make lugging a lot easier. I labeled each container with a laminated sign for each of my six classes.

The crucial aspect of organizing, however, is to make sure that what's inside a student's portfolio is orderly. Some might think "teenager and orderly" verge on paradoxical, but with proper instruction you'd be surprised. Most of the books are easy to go through. Simple things like dividers between sections and cover sheets save me time and the frustration of searching. At the beginning of the year just before "Portfolio Day," I hand out a sheet similar to Figure 7–5.

About two or three weeks into the new quarter, I hand out a letter to

Organizing Your 109 Portfolio

It's that time of year when the muffled screams of frustration ripple up and down the corridors of Mountain Valley High School. *Yes*, it's portfolio time in Room 109. Don't you just feel good all over?

Organizing your portfolio is a simple affair. Remember the ones you saw on the first day of class? Order and neatness are the rules of the day. Use dividers! Only include the work for this quarter . . . don't include 4,000 sheets of blank paper to make it look thick (Nice try). Here's how your portfolio should be put together:

1. Three--ring binder <u>with</u> dividers . . . journal books should be tucked inside somewhere...make sure your name is on it. If your journals were typed or are not in a notebook, just slip them in a separate section.

2. Your cover sheets and assessment sheets should be at the front. Fill out the <u>entire</u> cover sheet; *explain your projects thoroughly*. Remember: Mr. K fills out the assessment sheet . . . duh! Some people write an intro. letter and add a Table of Contents.

3. Put your *keeper letter* at the beginning of the portfolio.

4. Three formal papers and <u>then</u> their labeled drafts (e.g. first draft, second draft, etc.)

5. Two informal papers and <u>then</u> the labeled drafts.

6. Your ninety--minute written book project. Other book projects.

7. Extra stuff . . . editing sheets, letters, notes, etc.

8. Kent Handouts

If you have any questions, talk to the *Portfolio Master.* **:)**

Figure 7–5. Handout on Portfolios

remind students about the basic requirements and the portfolio due date. They already know all of this, but a written reminder keeps the "I-didn't-know-we-had-a-portfolio-due" comments to a bare minimum. I also send a letter at the beginning of the year to their *keepers* about basic requirements and due dates. Since a portfolio pedagogy is new to most, keeping everyone informed is crucial. Plus, if there are any complaints later on by *keepers* or students, I have these letters. In public school, as most of us have come to realize, accountability is important.

Reading Portfolios

"Now it's your turn," cracks Andi as she plops her portfolio into the 6/7 Blue laundry basket. "Hope your eyes fall out," she laughs.

"I love you, too."

She strides out of the room slapping the huge piece of paper hanging in the doorway. *It's Portfolio Day.*

Once again, organization is the key to this part of a portfolio classroom. I collect portfolios on a Friday. I do not accept late portfolios—unless of course the student has one of *those* excuses. A lost disk is not one of them. I am genuinely unforgiving when it comes to almost every excuse. It's their responsibility, plain and simple, and they know this from day one.

Normally, I have over one hundred portfolios to read and respond to. A few kids get them in early. A few. I read those immediately and award a bit of extra credit.

I compose my letter in response to each portfolio while I'm reading. I have a notebook computer, so that makes it convenient. I print out two copies of the response letter to keep a hard copy on file. Often, I will write one to four general paragraphs about the class as a whole and "paste" them into the beginning of individual letters (see "Evaluation" section later on). Then, I write specifically to that student. Writing about the class as a whole and about the student individually creates a balanced response.

I also take out the *keeper letter* at the beginning of the portfolio if it is addressed to me. If it's not, I might ask for a copy, just for my own research and thinking.

My kids know up front that I only read ten journal entries of the forty-eight. I select them at random—mostly by the title. I read each of the three formal and two informal papers; however, I only page through the rough drafts to look for genuine revision. If there's a question about revision, I compare each draft. (This is not fun.)

As you can see by the response letters I've included thus far, I will write about anything, from certain aspects of their writing to their attitude in class. I don't have a formula per se. It's whatever strikes me, and I try to make these letters as personal as possible. These young people deserve nothing less.

Here's how I schedule portfolio week:

Friday, *Portfolio Day*: I may have already read and responded to five or more portfolios by portfolio day. Friday evening, I read five more portfolios and then watch a movie where "destruction" is the theme.

Saturday: I begin reading at seven in the morning in the Writing Center at school. My goal for the day is fifteen portfolios. Some portfolios take twenty minutes to read and respond to; others take forty-five. Every once in a while I'll spend over an hour on a single portfolio. A couple each quarter take only five minutes to read, but ten minutes or more for response. These students need my best. At nine o'clock in the morning, twenty or so student readers show up at school (see "Student Responses" section later on). Each will read and respond to one to three portfolios. They stay until noon.

Sunday: Same as Saturday. I begin reading at seven and kids arrive at nine. By Sunday night I usually have forty or so portfolios completed.

Monday: My goal for weekdays is twelve portfolios a day. During this week, after portfolios are collected, I have minimal classroom responsibilities. Students are busy writing extensive reflections of the quarter (see "Student Reflections" section later on). The kids are almost always quiet during this week. I am a bit on edge, if you get my drift. They know when to leave me to myself. When I have completed an entire class of portfolios, I hang up a sign so those students can come by and pick them up. This stops kids from popping by asking, "Got mine done yet?"

IMPORTANT: Without a week of in-class reading time, I would not be able to read and respond to portfolios in the time allotted.

Tuesday–Friday: I read and respond to twelve portfolios each day.

Saturday: I read and respond to ten portfolios. (Student readers only work the first weekend.)

Sunday: I read and respond to ten portfolios.

Monday: The last of the portfolios are returned. I collect the quarter-end reflections. I won't begin reading them for a few days. Then I compile a synthesis of their comments.

(This year I experimented by picking up one class's portfolios each day during the final week of the marking period. I rotated which class would be first, second, and so on. I liked it. This procedure tempered the frenzy in our computer room and the Writing Center. But more, I was not overwhelmed on one day with one hundred or more portfolios and with the endless questions that always accompany portfolio day.)

By the time I have completed the reading, I'm tired. Yet, I bounce back. I am so energized by my students' work and by the work I did in response, I'm ready to go.

We begin the new quarter with discussions on a theme. Something new and inviting. Our discussions last for a week or longer—it always depends on the class. During this time, some kids get a bit ahead on journals; some may even begin papers. Most are searching for <u>the</u> book. As compared to what we have just finished, the next two weeks in Room 109 are relaxing in many ways for both the students and me.

But then, just as sure as the sun will rise, the next portfolio calls.

8

Assessment:
Telling the Story of a Portfolio

Evaluation: The Story of Learning

I used to grade everything. Rough drafts. Journals. Poems. Speeches. Even quarter-end evaluations and reflections.

Now I don't.

My first year I used to have from fifteen to twenty-five grades in my grade book for every quarter of the year.

Now there's only one.

Some grades were worth more than others. Two pop miniquizzes were worth a quiz. Four quizzes might have been worth one test. One term paper was worth three tests. The final exam equaled four tests, and the bonus question equaled a quiz grade, unless, of course, it was a take-home bonus question.

That doesn't happen anymore.

Evaluation helps my students learn. With the right words in my portfolio letter or during a conference, I can help my students understand their own strengths and weaknesses. And if I'm *really* good with my words, I can help them find their way to the next level of ability and understanding.

I am not alone in this process. Since students must have editors for their written work, they are continually receiving feedback. *Keeper* letters and student letters in response to the quarterly portfolios add to the process of assessing. Additionally, after the portfolios are turned in, students write reflections of themselves and their work. This self-assessment adds to the overall picture of the work.

By the end of the year, the students will have received up to twenty letters about their work and will have written up to fifty or more pages of reflection. Seeing one's work and, in a way, one's self through the eyes of many different people is a valuable learning experience. Think about all those letters and writings in response to one person's work; it beats the heck out of an eighty-three. What is an eighty-three, anyway?

At first, awarding only one grade at the end of the quarter made me nervous. It made students and parents nervous, too. But with time and good communication, there's barely a mention of grading now. The only real complaint I have experienced in the past five years—other than quibbling over a couple of points here or there—happened this year. One mom felt I was too generous with a grade. That was a first for me.

One important aspect of assessment for me: I am always in the process of thinking about and revising the way I present my understanding of my students' work. With the written responses, assessment sheets, conferences, and reflections, these young people get a clear picture of who they are as English students and, in some ways, who they are as people. Indeed, the purpose of evaluation is to help my students see themselves.

A Letter to Jami: A Teacher's Portfolio Response

Dear Jami,

Chill, Jami. Chill.

Everyone falls behind, gets a bit ahead, stays focused, then falls into the quagmire of being unfocused. That's life. Don't think about it so much. Just do. Great things happen when we just make a small move.

The opening of "Diversity" is sparkling. (Speaking of sparkling—the title needs a bit of oomph! Ha.) Telling your story of living in Nashua, N.H., helps us come to know more about difference. I loved the details in your work. These specifics make the piece believable. Beautiful. There are a number of technical problems in this (e.g., run-ons—see my marks on page two), but in the end it's a winning essay because it is honest and straightforward. It's a story of someone's trials. Having read this, I admire you even more.

"My Life" is a chorus. I enjoyed listening to the songs of you. It's amazing how we all have our different verses. Yours is remarkable. I love the way you have grown in other people's eyes. You've come a long way. "Memories of You" is brilliantly conceived and a wonderful sharing. Your mom was special to have written to you about your early years in this way. I'm sure it was difficult for her now that you and she live so far away from one another. I wonder—and don't feel

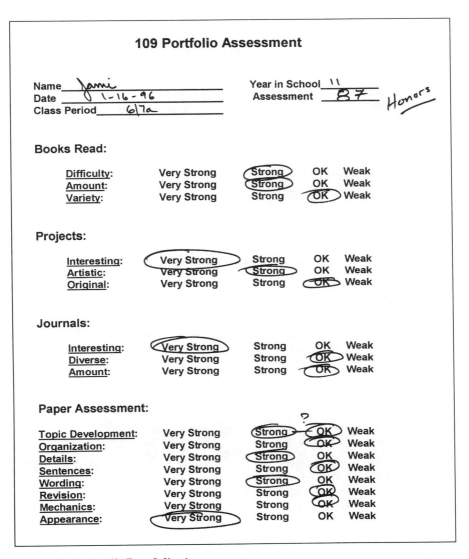

Figure 8–1. Jami's Portfolio Assessment

In-class Work & Participation in Room 109:

Use of time:	Very Strong	Strong	(OK)	Weak
Listener:	Very Strong	(Strong)	OK	Weak
Questioner:	Very Strong	(Strong)	OK	Weak
Speaker:	Very Strong	Strong	(OK)	Weak
Large Group:	Very Strong	Strong	(OK)	Weak
Small Group:	Very Strong	(Strong)	OK	Weak

Portfolio Appearance:

(Very Strong)   Strong   OK   Weak *Beautiful*

OVERALL ASSESSMENT:

Very Strong   (Strong)   OK   Weak

Additional Teacher Comments:

✓ When you use " " the commas and periods go inside the quotation

✓ They're = They are   ☺

✓ Try a more ... philosophical ... book. See me — more variety in reading.

✓ You might be using too many editors. Try one editor for the first 3 drafts then give it out to someone new. It's got to be confusing to have 3 different people commenting on your first draft ??

✓ Keep smiling!   ☺

Figure 8–1. Continued

at all pressured—if I could have a copy of this section? I admire this essay and might like to write a bit about it. Let me know. Thanks.

"Ethics" and "Boredom" are quickies on your part, but I certainly understand—after reading your other essays—why that's so. Nice work for what's here, but we both know you've got "a better." Interesting perspectives throughout. Work on one for next quarter?

It's also interesting how you list your journal entry titles as a table of contents. Amazing . . . your journal is so much a *book of you.*

Thanks for your work in 109. I hope you're happy with yourself. You are a good and decent person, Jami. I'm glad you're here.

> YLET,
> Rich Kent

When we focus on a theme like acting, I devise a specific comment sheet that will serve as an addendum to the regular assessment page and letter responses. The students enjoy and learn from my individual comments about their presentations. These sheets also help me stay specific when chatting about a particular presentation. In addition, all students are given an assessment sheet of their own so they can write about their various performances. I find the students' comments about themselves to be honest and direct. Writing reflectively about their time "on stage" serves as one more learning tool.

In my individual portfolio letter responses at the end of Stage 109, I often write two or so general paragraphs about each class. I save these paragraphs in my computer and paste them into each student's letter. Here's an example of those general paragraphs to a class that had brilliant presentations but were not so good at listening:

First, some general comments about the plays and presentations. Needless to say there were some memorable presentations in 3/4 B. I loved the improvisations, both in large and small groups. People were playful and fun. What a time! From *Annie* to *Who's on First?* to *Much Ado About Nothing* . . . Yes, indeed, what a time.

If I had one complaint, it might be that I don't think we were always the best audience we could be. It's hard to sit and watch. Believe me, I sit and watch and listen *all day long,* so I know how difficult it is. It's important to work hard to give support and to solicit the best performances from the actors. This is our job in the audience. Next time you are sitting through a presentation or a

Stage 109
3rd Quarter
Comment and Assessment Sheet

Name *Linda*   Class *4.2A*   Year in School *10th*

Introduction
Comment: I'm surprised I wasn't nervous. I did a
pretty good job.

Show 'n Tell Presentation
Comment: I thought I was going to cry. My aunt Tracy
will always be my favorite.

Poem
Comment: I only read this 3 times out loud. I stunk. Sorry. I
shouldn't have chose such a scary poem.

A Reading from a novel or short story
Comment: When I read this last year, it made me sick. I
knew I wanted to do it here. I practiced hard. I

Solo Improvisation
Comment: I felt like a little kid with the magic wand.
It seemed easy. I did well.

Group Improvisation
Comment: We really had fun. I've never been so **comfortable**.
George is CRAZY!

Group Play
Comment: We worked hard on this. It came together at
Marcy's house. I hope you liked it!

You as a listener and audience
Comment: Most peoples' presentations were cool. I liked
to listen. I didn't like to spend time listening
to those plays that were not practiced. You know
what I mean. All in all it's been a great 3 weeks.

Figure 8–2. Student Comment and Assessment Sheet on Presentations

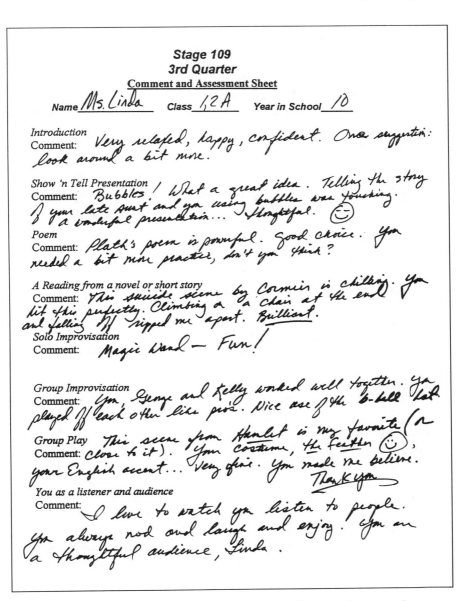

Stage 109
3rd Quarter
<u>**Comment and Assessment Sheet**</u>

Name *Ms. Linda*   Class *12 A*   Year in School *10*

Introduction
Comment: *Very relaxed, happy, confident. One suggestion: look around a bit more.*

Show 'n Tell Presentation
Comment: *Bubbles! What a great idea. Telling the story of your late aunt and you using bubbles was touching. A wonderful presentation... Thoughtful.* 😊

Poem
Comment: *Plath's poem is powerful. Good choice. You needed a bit more practice, don't you think?*

A Reading from a novel or short story
Comment: *This suicide scene by Cormier is chilling. You hit this perfectly. Climbing on a chair at the end and falling off ripped me apart. Brilliant.*

Solo Improvisation
Comment: *Magic Wand — Fun!*

Group Improvisation
Comment: *You, George and Kelly worked well together. You played off each other like pros. Nice use of the b-ball hat.*

Group Play
Comment: *This scene from Hamlet is my favorite (a close 2nd). Your costume, the feather* 😊 *, your English accent... Very fine. You made me believe. Thank you*

You as a listener and audience
Comment: *I love to watch you listen to people. You always nod and laugh and enjoy. You are a thoughtful audience, Linda.*

Figure 8–3. Teacher Comment and Assessment Sheet on Presentations

lecture or a play, remember to give the folks on stage your very best in response.

These general comments help me push one or two instructional points for the benefit of the entire class.

I have just recently devised an assessment sheet for my poetry students' portfolios. I'm still in the process of fine-tuning this. To be truthful, I am not sure this instrument is necessary. Time and my students will tell.

Along with these assessment sheets are reaction letters written by me and one of their poetry classmates. From reading these responses, I believe these young poets begin to understand my, or our, understanding of their work. Then, if all goes well, they begin the trek to the next level as poets.

The following is a poetry portfolio reaction letter.

Dear Michelle,

You are a working poet.

The level of commitment and passion you show toward poetry is astounding. Each day you share poems that you've written or read. Each day you listen intently to your colleagues in class as they read and talk. You write with a love for nature that is extraordinary. I admire you, Michelle.

The word choice in "Wolves" creates many vivid images. I see these pictures clearly as I read your poem. This is a playful piece, one that makes us want to take a hike into the wilderness and live among the wolves. A fine poem, Michelle.

"The Lioness" shows us the reality of the natural world. What comes to mind when I read this poem is a quotation by Robert Green Ingersoll from *Some Reasons Why*: "In nature there are neither rewards nor punishments—there are consequences." There is no sentimentality in this poem. Survival of the fittest, or natural selection, is simply the way of the African plains. You show us with your skillful diction that we should not feel sorry—we should simply accept. I appreciate your poem "The Lioness" for its straightforward reporting of nature.

I loved looking through your works-in-progress. This is truly the journal of one who cares deeply about poetry. So much is happening in this portfolio. The organization and the focus of your songs is stunning; the deliberate work of seeking out those "best words" through multiple revisions is unmistakable. Further, your

Dead Poets Society
Assessment

Name_____   Year in School_____

Date _____   Assessment _____

Class Period **Lunch**

DPS Chapbook Poem:

Title: _____

Final Poem:	**Very Strong**	**Strong**	**OK**	**Weak**
Revision:	**Very Strong**	**Strong**	**OK**	**Weak**

Top Five Poems Assessed:

Titles: _____   _____

_____   _____

_____

Theme Development:	**Very Strong**	**Strong**	**OK**	**Weak**
Organization:	**Very Strong**	**Strong**	**OK**	**Weak**
Details:	**Very Strong**	**Strong**	**OK**	**Weak**
Lines:	**Very Strong**	**Strong**	**OK**	**Weak**
Wording:	**Very Strong**	**Strong**	**OK**	**Weak**
Sound Quality:	**Very Strong**	**Strong**	**OK**	**Weak**
Genuine Revision:	**Very Strong**	**Strong**	**OK**	**Weak**
Mechanics:	**Very Strong**	**Strong**	**OK**	**Weak**
Appearance:	**Very Strong**	**Strong**	**OK**	**Weak**
Use of metaphor:	**Very Strong**	**Strong**	**OK**	**Weak**
Use of Imagery:	**Very Strong**	**Strong**	**OK**	**Weak**

Figure 8–4. Assessment Sheet for Poetry Students' Portfolios

In-class Work & Participation in DPS:

<u>Use of time</u>:	Very Strong	Strong	OK	Weak
<u>Listener</u>:	Very Strong	Strong	OK	Weak
<u>Questioner</u>:	Very Strong	Strong	OK	Weak
<u>Speaker</u>:	Very Strong	Strong	OK	Weak
<u>Large Group</u>:	Very Strong	Strong	OK	Weak
<u>Small Group</u>:	Very Strong	Strong	OK	Weak
<u>Friday Readings</u>:	Very Strong	Strong	OK	Weak

Books Read, either partially or wholly, for DPS:

_____

_____

_____

_____

OVERALL ASSESSMENT:

Very Strong   Strong   OK   Weak

Kent's Comments:

_____

_____

_____

_____

Figure 8–4. Continued

participation in class is that of a leader. You show all of us what it is to be a student of poetry. Indeed, you show us what it is to be a poet.

Congratulations. I'm proud of you, Michelle.

Your Loving English Teacher,

For me, one of the most important books in English education has been *What Is English?* by Peter Elbow. This reflection of the 1987 English Coalition Conference illuminates many of the issues teachers face. At Bread Loaf, many of us packed into a classroom in the Barn to hear Elbow's views on evaluation, grading, and our hunger to rank people.

Elbow (1986) also writes about the power of portfolio assessment as a way to learn:

> Portfolio assessment helps the learning climate because it reinforces continuing effort and improvement: it encourages students to try to revise and improve poor work rather than to feel punished or to give up because of the poor work they started with. It gets away from a "putting in time" model for learning and instead makes for a more forward-pointing dynamic of "building toward your best" (167).

(I bought six copies of this book for my English colleagues at Mountain Valley High School. The issues expressed—debates on the literary canon, goals and testing, teaching grammar in context, and so on—created the focus for two years of discussions within our department during my tenure as chairperson. For over a year, we met for two to three hours once a month on a Sunday to chat and argue, discuss and share. Sadly, we have discontinued this practice. Yet my memories of those gatherings remain some of my best as a teacher.)

One thing I know for sure about grading portfolios in Room 109: my students and I usually agree—within a few points—on the final number. There's no mystery and little debate. After developing one portfolio, kids figure out the standards. They also know they are in charge of their ultimate grade.

During a presentation at the University of Maine at Farmington, Kathy summed up her 109 portfolio experience this way:

> *This is my rank card. It tells you with numbers how a teacher thought I did with their work. This is my portfolio. It shows you with words and ideas what I think and what other people think of me and my work.*

Portfolios and parent/teacher conferences

One more thing about portfolios: It's a lot easier to talk about a child's English performance with his or her *keeper* when a package of student work sits in front of us. During parent/teacher conferences, portfolios help center and balance the conversation.

Keepers who wish can also keep closer track of their children's English work throughout the quarter by periodically looking at the portfolio. Because of my initial letter, *keepers* are well aware of the portfolio requirements.

Questions About Portfolios

Does anyone ever fail? This isn't *Never-never land.*

> Dear Robert,
>   When I picked up your portfolio, I smiled. I figured you'd really done it up just like you promised last quarter. But once I started looking closely . . . well, you know the rest of the story.
>   For me, one of the tough parts of teaching is telling someone I like that they're not cutting it. That's what I've got to say to you. It's easy for me to say nice things about the person you are. You're a good guy with a wonderful personality, but I'm not doing you any favors by ignoring the facts about you as a student.
>   At our mid-quarter interview you assured me that you were well on your way with your portfolio. You even listed the stuff you had done and were organizing. But now I can tell you weren't being honest. In your portfolio you listed four papers, two formals and two informals. Here's what's really in your portfolio:
>
> "Infinity, Where should I begin?"
>   This paper has numerous rough drafts, so it's formal.
>
> "Being behind sucks"
>   This is informal—there are *no* drafts and it has numerous mistakes. It also has no concluding paragraph.
>
> "Did I miss out?"
>   Again, this is an informal as there are no drafts. In fact, this paper is

almost exactly like one of your journal entries from last quarter. I remember you talking about this subject in a couple of your journal entries.

As you can see, there are two informals and one formal. The requirements are three formals and two informals.

You have written thirty of the forty-eight journal entries. They are all day-to-day diary entries and most are around seventy-five words, not 150. We talked about your journals last quarter. I am glad that you're writing, but you should look to focus on different ideas. It's not that I mind hearing about your daily life; it's just not the point of this type of writing. *But you already know this because we've talked before.*

Your class participation is good. Your ideas are interesting; you're kind to people in class; you're generally a good listener. I appreciate your input and encourage you to volunteer just a bit more. With just a little effort, you could be a class leader.

Projects. As you know, you're supposed to produce three to five projects. Your one project—a poster over FNL—doesn't meet the requirements for class.

I know you don't enjoy reading, but somehow you've got to do it. Reading only one book, *Friday Night Lights,* is not an acceptable amount of reading for a young man who's talking a lot about going to college. College requires an immense amount of high-level reading. Will you be able to do that? Not if you don't practice. In English, you have the opportunity to choose what you'd like to read; that's a pretty good situation. You *must* improve the amount of reading you do for this next half year.

Last quarter you received a 78 for your work. This quarter you have failed with a 65. You and I both know that you could kick this class in the butt if you applied yourself. You and I both know that you could be receiving honors grades. However . . .

I wrote this because I know how successful you could be. Now, you need to make some choices. You're a senior so no one's going to hold your hand. No one's going to scream and yell at you. It's all in your hands. My suggestion? *Work.* Read every day. Write every day. Don't waste time during workshop by chatting with people. Work on the weekends. Most of all, don't fool yourself. Whatever you decide to do, take the responsibility for your actions.

If you continue to work like this you might not get into college. If you do get in and work like this, you'll waste your money and end up flunking out. Does it have to be this way? Absolutely not. You can be anything you want, Robert. *Anything.*

I'm here to help you. I'm in school every morning at 7:00 A.M. I will stay after school every night for anyone. I can't do any more. *It's your turn.*

YLET,
Rich Kent

Does anyone ever cheat? Ditto.

Dear Mr. Kent,

I feel very guilty for what I have done. It was wrong, and I can't believe that I tried to trick you. I want you to believe that all the papers in my portfolio were originally written this year. I have excluded all work that shouldn't have been there in the first place.

I would like to take this time to apologize to you. I always used to be the best English student in the class. When I found out that I was going to have to read five books, and I only read two and a half, I panicked. I thought my only alternative was to try to get away with a stunt like that. I'm sorry.

So now, I would like to turn in my portfolio the way it is. I hope that you will accept it. I worked very hard on my papers and tried to read as much as I could. It is extremely difficult to read five books in one quarter, when last year we didn't read five books in one year. I know I belong in this class. I love this class, you know that.

I hope you can still respect me as your student and friend. Just give me a chance in here to prove myself, that's all I ask of you.

Sincerely,
R.

Keeper Letters

The day I required my students to share their portfolios with a parent, guardian, or significant adult in their lives (a.k.a. *keepers*), my practice began moving to another level.

It's funny to look back at the time before the *keepers* took an active role in portfolio response. Back when my words and my one-page assessment sheet were my young colleagues' only feedback at the end of each quarter. Now, those responses alone seem flat, lacking in balance, and incomplete. Perhaps worst of all, I feel my former students and their *keepers* missed out on something special.

When I first announced this requirement and passed out a letter to be taken home (now my practice is to mail this letter home at the beginning of the year), some of the kids groaned. "I don't want her to read my journals."

"Share what you can," I said, attempting to prevent a mass revolt. Most settled in with the fact that their folks—or whoever—were going to be a part of this portfolio adventure. A few, like August, came to me privately.

"Could I have my sister write about my portfolio?" she asked.

This young mother explained that her autobiography was too direct and that her mom wouldn't handle it well.

Andrea's parents were working in New York. She asked her special education teacher, Deb Brown, to write. Out of my 120 students, ten asked someone other than a parent or guardian to write a response. Eight more simply didn't fulfill the requirement. The *keeper* letters were placed at the front of the portfolio.

Portfolio week:

"My mother worked for three days on her letter, Mr. Kent," laughed Suzie.

"Mine thinks she's some kind of creative writer," moaned Jason, embarrassed by the playfulness in his mom's wonderful letter.

"Ha! My father sat with a dictionary and looked up every word over five letters!" announced Shelly.

And so the reports of the *keepers'* labors came forth in class after class. Though they would not admit it outright, my sense was that most of these young people enjoyed their *keepers'* participation.

Dear Mr. Kent:

After reading Pam's portfolio, it is difficult to describe the gamut of emotions that it has evoked for me . . . Pain, sorrow, sadness, admiration, laughter and hope.

Pain and sorrow that any young person should have to experience what she has so far in her young life.

Admiration for your ability and rapport that allows students to look within themselves and express feelings that might otherwise be buried and labeled unimportant. You are the first person to whom Pam has openly expressed over two years of intense emotions that have been building. For that, I am grateful to you.

Laughter to recall the July 4th Wilderness Expedition and curiosity to read the other three versions!

Hope, that she will continue to gain confidence and growth with your writing and reading challenges. Hope, that she will continue to express all her emotions through her writing. Hope, that she will recognize the critical need for writing skills for tomorrow's success . . . And hope that next quarter, I get more time to review this collection.

Thanks for your dedication, Lynn S.

My dearest Son,
My rising sun,

Congratulations, YOU have produced a fantastic portfolio! Certainly your work is engaging, entertaining, suspenseful and honest. I really enjoyed your autobiography and your candid version of small town life.

When I read your "Simple Lessons" story I was filled with so many emotions. First came pride in my insightful and intelligent son. Next was awe that a person of fifteen years could have learned so many valuable and endearing lessons. Then sadness that I didn't learn these lessons "early enough"—but fulfilled that my son did! Finally LOVE, love, love was all consuming. Vic LeClaire was a genuinely caring young man with the qualities and heart to keep humankind afloat. You have the ability to revitalize people and give them insight—this is a rare gift.

You have worked very hard on this masterpiece and should be proud. Your writing is creative and a pleasure to read.

Keep writing,
P.S. I love your sense of humor!   Love Mom

It struck me as I reread the collection of letters, that this was, perhaps, the first time these adults had ever looked closely at and written about their child's schoolwork. I could sense that this exercise brought most of these folks to a new level of understanding, both as parent/guardian and as a former English student.

From the parent-guardian side, Nancy D. says it best. "Hey, this is my kid here! I'm getting a wide-open look straight into his eighteen-year-old head. Scary! Wonderful! And very special." It is a "look" that we language arts and writing teachers live with each day. An intimate, up-close look that sometimes I have taken for granted. Sharing this opportunity with these adults opened up one more valuable avenue for communication. I could only imagine some of the dinner table conversations.

I would venture to say that teachers (no matter the subject area) who use *writing to learn* discover more about their students as people from their manuscripts than through daily classroom discussions. This sharing—like reading autobiographies and journals—helps build the kind of relationship necessary for effective teaching and vital learning. This is especially true when the teacher responds in writing to a student's work.

Furthermore, as former English students, the *keepers* were once again confronted with a writing assignment. I know the old juices began to churn once they read my letter. This was evident in Liz A.'s note to me at the bottom of her letter in Josh's portfolio:

> PS My level of awareness and appreciation for Josh's work increased when you, in effect, added a single pronoun to this quarter's guides and info sheets. Hearing myself telling Josh, "*you* have to write" was pretty easy compared to looking at this paper thinking "*I* have to write." (Rough draft not included!)

Sis H. writes openly, "Writing has never come easy to me." And Robert D. admits, "I'm sure my paper probably needs to be edited at least a few times!"

Most of the *keepers* are amazed at the work it takes to develop a 109 portfolio. Wayne G. hit it square by emphasizing the "decision making, time management and organizational skills" that are required of his son, Tim. Some parents, like Lynn's mom Jane, had a clear message for me: "Want to let you know that Lynn has worked very hard on her portfolio. I myself think she has done a very good job."

As a teacher researcher, I am constantly studying Room 109 and soliciting input. Students offer suggestions in their quarter-end reflections. Evaluations from administrators, visits from university teachers and students, and conversations with colleagues have all helped me look closely and make more informed decisions about what we do.

And now the *keepers*. Their letters offer me an opportunity to see my practice from far beyond the classroom walls. Most of these letters come from the kitchen tables of my students. There, the forces of caring, commitment, and love help us see more clearly.

A Keeper Synthesis

Once a year, usually after the first portfolio, I compile a synthesis of *keeper* comments and mail them home. Of everything that comes out of Room 109, this might be the most popular. Normally, these collections are six or seven pages long. Here's a sampling of comments.

> Dear Keepers of the Students of 109,
>
> Your letters in response to the 109ers' English portfolios made me think and helped me learn. The insight, sensitivity, and humor within your comments had me laughing one moment and stilled in thought the next. Thank you for your efforts.
>
> Responses ranged from single paragraphs to a couple of pages. (Some could have been formal papers!) Mothers and fathers, uncles and aunts, sisters, friends, and special teachers wrote the remarks for our students. No matter the length of the comment, meaning was conveyed.
>
> Because these letters and notes helped all of us in 109, I must share some of the writing with you. I have not asked permission to do this, so I won't include the names of the authors or last names of the students. *(You need to know, some of the letters were directed to the student, others were written to me.)* The following collection helps the reader come to know . . . in the end, this is the way we make meaning of experience.

Life Moments from Portfolio Responses

As I reviewed Lindy's portfolio my first thought was "Is this my kid?"

When Jon decided to join your class I was very leery because my dear son is a professional procrastinator.

Crack the whip, Mr. Kent!

Taking into account all the reading, the writing, the edits, this portfolio has been quite a challenge for your mind. Now it's time to go out and buy more ink for the word processor!

Portfolios, oh . . . the parent's nightmare. I've come to think of them right up there with yeast infections and root canals.

You give students a "gift" of life. You encourage & strengthen their individuality.

I see remarkable improvement in your writing fluency, coherence, and clarity.

I just finished reading my sister's portfolio. I think it's great!

I trudged up stairs planning to hit the sack. I spotted your note to read your work . . . I was instantly awake and read for the next hour. I laughed and I cried. You took me through a whole gamut of emotions.

At home she can be introverted, but reading these papers helps us see her even more than ever.

Thanks for asking me to review this. I have enjoyed it, learned from it and laughed a lot while I was doing it!

By reading through his papers I was able to have a clearer understanding of what is really happening in the heart of my child.

Thanks for sharing more of you with me . . . I love you.

Is there much else that could be said? Thank you for sharing these moments with me. I feel privileged to have been included in these exchanges.

I look forward to meeting you during parent/teacher conferences on Thursday, November 9th, from 11 A.M. to 7 P.M. To find Room 109, take a right in the main lobby and walk half way down the corridor until you hear Chopin playing softly . . . we're just on the right.

Warmly,
Rich Kent, Teacher

Student Responses to Portfolios

On the Saturday and Sunday mornings after portfolios are turned in, twenty or so of my students show up on the front steps of Mountain Valley High School. Many are carrying Dunkin' Donuts coffee mugs or twenty-ounce bottles of soda. For the next three or four hours, they will read and respond in writing to their fellow students' portfolios. Each student reads one to three portfolios and writes a response of one or two pages. On rare occasions, when a student can't make a weekend session—perhaps they live too far out of town and have no way in—I allow them to take three portfolios home with them overnight. I don't advertise this.

When I first began this practice, most of the readers came from the Writing Center class; they were awarded extra credit for their weekend work. Now, all of my students are required to read and respond to portfolios once during the year. Everyone deserves this opportunity.

As with the *keeper* letter, this peer response helps my students—both reader and writer—learn more about writing and thinking.

Here's one paragraph from Darcy's letter to Dan. I love how she simultaneously encourages and compliments, suggests and instructs. Darcy is a sophomore and Dan is a junior.

> Dear Dan,
>
> I take it you had an interesting time building your log cabin? By reading your paper I got a clearer picture of Roger, Jason and you out there in the woods trying to build that cabin. I would love to see your pictures. The paper itself is good. However, you might want to "widen your horizon" on editors. There were a few grammar and spelling mistakes that your computer failed to pick up. Next time you might also want to have another person look over your work as well. Your independent project paper was filled with valuable information for anybody wanting to go out and create a cabin in the woods. It was information like this that helped create a more visual aspect to the paper. Hope you had fun . . .
>
> Darcy

Darcy's advice is clear: Use editors. She expresses the potentiality of Dan's piece while pointing out the strengths. Hers is a balanced, thoughtful approach.

Yes, there were times when kids went over the deep end with their comments: "You know, my fourth grade sister writes better than you." These types of comments have been minimized or eliminated since I've begun explaining my expectations to the entire Saturday/Sunday morning crew at once. I use the "fourth grade sister" comment as a prime example of what *not* to do. I also hang up a couple of posters with certain guidelines:

The Golden Rules of Reading and Responding to a Classmate's Portfolio

- Be kind and conversational—don't act like a know-it-all.
- Point out strengths.
- Focus on strongest, most effective paper.

- Comment on overall portfolio—relate it to your experiences with portfolios.
- Make simple suggestions for improvement.
- How are their revisions?
- Did their editors make good suggestions?
- Technical stuff: If they make the same mistake a lot, let them know.
- I always find it easier to type my responses while I am reading along.

I ask for copies of these letters for the *People Plan* files, and then I glance through them to make sure the responses aren't hurtful or inappropriate. This only takes a few minutes.

Often, these peer responses go a long way in helping my less able students feel hopeful and respected.

Dear Robert,
   After reading your portfolio, I immediately thought of my sophomore year. I didn't really care about school or anything. It was just fine with me to get by . . . I think you could really have a good portfolio if you put in some more time and energy. You have to find something that excites you and is fun to write about. Write a paper about your favorite band or sport or one of your hobbies. If you have trouble finding the right words to make your papers good, don't worry, that's what editing is for.
                                                                Brian

Here, a highly respected student-athlete named Brian works to encourage a young man who has experienced little success in school or out. I watched as Robert read the letters he received and knew Brian's words made a difference. The next quarter, Robert worked harder and produced more.

Here's part of a fine example by Jeremy:

Katie,
   Your portfolio for this first quarter was truly captivating.
   Your papers show a marvelous level of expressiveness. You are building a broad and solid foundation in this first level of writing. I would love to come back two years from now and read your work. I guarantee you will even amaze yourself.

You have brought to light the value of friendships for yourself. You have a gift for reflecting on special memories and extracting from them exactly what it is that made those moments special. It is important to reflect and grow on the past.

"Katie-Kins," "It's a Girl Thing," and "Pink and Yellow Petticoats" are moving for the reader. They allow them to enter your life and live the moments over with you. You convey your feelings well in your writing. It was a unique experience for me to read about a little girl growing up, because I, of course, was a little boy. Your writing was a fine opportunity for me to expand my knowledge of the way different people mature and the way the opposite sex thinks.

This is truly a fine portfolio. It does show a great deal of time spent and a remarkable level of thinking. The motives behind your papers are genuine, and a few technical errors and bits of overwriting don't take away from them at all (just to give you something to think about for next quarter).

> Your friend,
> Jeremy

A senior student, Jeremy exhibits confidence in Katie and, perhaps more important, in himself. He freely compliments specific pieces of her writing. "Truly captivating," "marvelous level of expressiveness," "two years from now . . . you will even amaze yourself." As I read his comments, I knew how encouraged Katie, a sophomore, must have felt. As a teacher, Jeremy is skillful at helping this student see the power of her own writing.

In the midst of his thoughtful letter, Jeremy gently instructs that "a few technical errors and bits of overwriting . . . give you something to think about for next quarter." Truly, this is one writer speaking to another. No judgments, nothing harsh, no red-pen blood trails. His words are personal, direct, and considerate. What writer, student or professional, wouldn't want Jeremy to write him or her a letter?

The Letters of One Portfolio

His research paper on the moon revealed his scholarship. The painting he presented in celebration of his research combined rich, moody colors in a tapestry of meaning. His vampire poem illustrated his humor. Indeed, this collection represented Josh well.

I believe wholeheartedly in inclusion and have enjoyed many different learners over my career. Integrating Josh, a boy with Down's Syndrome, into Room 109 helped me in many ways. Most of all, I learned more about levels of scholarship and about individual standards. I also discovered one more way to define *joy* . . . so did Josh's classmates in Period 6/7 Silver.

All twenty-three pairs of eyes were turned toward my desk in the corner of the room. Josh—clearly the most popular kid in class for his endearing smile, his infectious laugh, and his high fives generously shared with everyone—sat with me reviewing his first-quarter portfolio. His most effective piece, an autobiography, showed his sensitivities and love of family. In the body of his essay, the line "Everybody in my family has Down's Syndrome" remains a powerful metaphor of life and living for me. Even more, his words speak mightily about his special family. As with many successful children, family plays the critical role in Josh's life.

At the end of each interview, I ask my students to "ball park" their portfolio grade within five points. They are not grading themselves. It's a reality check; a way of taking the conversations and personal letters about their portfolios and miraculously turning them into a number grade. Except for Josh, I can't remember the last time a student's grade and my final assessment didn't come within five points of one another.

"So, Josh. How do you think you did? What would you give yourself for a grade, give or take five points?"

His classmate friends, each with an ear turned toward this private conference, shifted in anticipation. Josh straightened up. A wide grin came to his face as he lifted his chin and straightened his shoulders. "A-plus!" he announced.

His fans exploded with cheers as Josh, quite pleased with his pronouncement, looked me square in the eye. I had no choice. I leaned over to him, smiling kindly, and whispered, "Not a chance, Josh. Not this time."

Indeed, among other items, I had the feeling Josh could write more than the twenty-eight journal entries he presented. After thoroughly reading his portfolio and responding with a letter, I assessed his performance as an honors grade of eighty-five.

Once all the letters of one portfolio are combined, a story unfolds. Here are the letters surrounding Josh's work for first quarter.

Dear Josh,

What a great guy you are! I love your smile and your polite way. I like the way you work and the way you treat Mrs. Brown. You're a great spirit to have in Room 109. You are as kind as your brother, Neil. I feel lucky to know you.

Your "Summer Mind" essay is wonderful. You have captured exactly the idea of thinking and being in the summer mind that Wallace Stevens spoke of. It is playful and personal. You have had a fun time with this piece, and it shows. Congratulations.

Thank you for sharing your time at the Norlands Historical Center. This paper gives me good details about the trip. You tell me about the people you went with and the things you saw. My favorite line of yours is, "She said if we didn't listen she would hit us on the head with her finger. Not a good picture." Funny! And it tells me that this was a serious experience at Norlands. You really learned about the history of school and the history of working on a farm years ago. Nice stuff, Josh.

Your journal entries are fun. Next quarter I think you should be able to do a few more. You talked about a lot of different things in your life; this way you kept my interest as a reader. "A Vampire Poem" is a great poem for Halloween. The best part for me is that you scared us all through the poem and then ended with "Don't worry . . . it's not real!!" That shows you are a sensitive person. Thanks!

The projects that you presented were fun. I'm happy that you did such creative things. Next quarter we'll look for more of the same.

That's it! Good work, Josh. Thanks for being the special person you are.

Your loving English Teacher,
Rich Kent

P.S. I hope you enjoy Dusty's letter to you. He's from Peru, too.

Dear Josh,

I think that you like to write. Am I right? I like how you wrote on topics that you find interesting. I also find the writing very thoughtful.

The paper on the moon was good. You seem to like the moon. I especially liked the part about thinking the moon is a piece of cheese. If you look at it for a moment it actually does resemble a big round piece of cheese. Have you ever noticed the face on the moon, and better yet, the rabbit riding the bike? The second one is a little harder to find, but most people will show you.

By what I have read, you liked your trip to the Norlands. I've been there before. It is a really neat place. It seems as if you had a lot of fun.

I enjoyed reading your autobiography. I think it is great how you expressed your feelings towards your family. You really love your family, as I do mine.

Your poem about vampires was different. I like poetry. I think that poetry is a great way to express things you love, or even just enjoy talking about.

Josh, you are a good writer. I enjoyed reading your portfolio. It's great that you are taking this class. I think you will have a lot of fun in the next three quarters of the year.

A friend,
Dusty H.

The following letter from Josh's parents appeared in the front of his portfolio:

Dear Mr. Kent,

I'm truly grateful that my literary masterpiece isn't due today! In its place, I will gladly offer my general comments!

We were tentatively hopeful that Josh might be able to handle some mainstream courses in H.S. We were also tentatively hopeful that some teachers could respond to him w/ positive acceptance in the classroom. We were elated to hear that he was enrolled in your class! I don't think he could have begun building a more positive self-image in any other mainstream environment.

Josh has always loved books and reading. The individualized format is great for him. He can participate from his own ability level and in his preferred interest areas and be with students who are all doing that as well. It's very personalized, yet all inclusive.

It's difficult for Josh to analyze and extract structural components, and abstracts elude him. With Mrs. Brown's help, he's making headway transferring his reading to correlated writing skills. The quantity of his writing is surprising as is another new skill development. Multiple drafts and editing are a big step forward. Typically, he would only do one assignment one time and that's it, no more, it's done. Being more attentive to how it's done and how to improve it is a pretty big deal!

He likes this "109," he's comfortable w/ the class (and the couch from time to time, I hear). With Josh we tend to view most possibilities as tentatively hopeful. I think he's willing to apply himself here. His gains and the rapport in your class are giving him a good foundation to try another step.

With great appreciation for you that has grown over these past ten years . . .

Sincerely,
Liz & Gary A.

Dusty received the following note in the mail:

Dear Dusty,

I wanted to take a moment to thank you for your kind words and encouraging thoughts in your letter to Joshua.

You gave him something of great personal value.

Just seeing his face when he read me your letter gave me a memory I'll always keep.

Congratulations on a *fantastic* soccer season! We wish you the very best in every endeavor you undertake!

May your kindness be returned and multiplied . . .

Sincerely,
Liz & Gary A.

This full circle of responses brought out the best in all of us. When rereading these letters as a collection, I thought back to my first year of teaching when all I offered up to my students' work was a number grade and a few short lines of instruction, encouragement, or congratulations. It is clear that the personal nature of portfolio assessment through letters enriches all participants in many varied ways. Surely, as Linda Rief (1992) writes in *Seeking Diversity*, students "want response to what they write. They want that response to be a dialogue—a confirmation of what they know in a conversational tone" (55).

In some cases students and *keepers* struggle with issues of privacy and performance. In this age of their initiation into adulthood, some teenagers simply don't want the adult(s) in their lives involved. Fair enough. However, even in refusing access to their work, at the very least the students are speaking about writing, about English, and about themselves with some adult who matters other than the teacher. They confront the issues. I'll take this dialogue over silence any day of the week. Over time, my experience has been that most students allow at least part of their portfolios to be reviewed and commented on. Only in rare cases have the *keepers* refused to respond.

Throughout the year, Josh taught all of his classmates a variety of lessons on scholarship and humor, acceptance and diversity. They were lessons well learned. By the end of the year, all of us in Period 6/7 Silver had Down's Syndrome, too. And happily so.

People Plans

This year, our school district's administration required all building principals to check the lesson plans of each teacher once a month. Each staff member's plan had to show how lessons connected with our district's curriculum. Initially, this resulted in a tedious maze for many, including me. With themes, individualized portfolios, and all the rest that goes along with managing a responsive classroom, developing traditional lesson plans would have been difficult at best.

My solution? *People Plans.* I created a file for each student, much like the files that doctors keep for their patients. Inside, I place copies of my letters, *keeper* letters, student letters, and other relevant material from each student's portfolio. I also have my own file for copies of general class letters, minilesson notes, and ideas for themes.

At the end of each quarter, I have the students look through the letters in their files and underline the instructional points that connect to our school's curriculum. For English/Language Arts that means locating comments about reading, writing, listening, speaking, viewing, observing, presenting, and all the rest. In a way, as you will see, this is like having an interactive lesson plan.

Remember the letter I wrote to Lindy in response to her autobiography? That ended up in her file. Here's one passage:

"I would love to see you take chances with your reading this year. You have a great deal to learn from books . . . all of us do. Let's challenge you; let's see if we can move you to another level as a reader."

In her response to me she wrote:

"Taking chances with my reading is very scary . . . but I'm up for the challenge."

In her folder, Lindy highlighted both passages and wrote "reading" in the right-hand margin. After reviewing the portfolio letters, each student writes one to three goals for the upcoming ranking period and places them in the *People Plan* file. Not surprisingly, Lindy wrote "I would seriously like to bring up my reading level" as one of her goals. Throughout the first half of the year, Lindy and I searched out more challenging books for her to read. By the end of the first semester, she wrote, "I'm proud of what I've accomplished with my reading."

For my principal, this package—a small, plastic, luggable file case—creates a picture of Room 109's curriculum, describes the individualized approach we're taking with each student, and shows how we're meeting our district's standards. Indeed, *People Plans* take a little bit of time and organization. However, and most important, this practice enables the student and the teacher to work cooperatively in an effort to focus on and improve the student's weaknesses.

9

Classroom Research: Coming to Know My Students and Myself

"Coming to Know" is borrowed from my Bread Loaf class with Dixie Goswami and James Britton. Back then, I was baffled by the notion of classroom research. A year after the class, I began reading *Students Teaching, Teachers Learning* (Branscombe et al. 1992), a book on teacher research as shared inquiry. I remember reading the title of the book over and over before opening it. Once I read the first paragraph, I began to understand and "name" what was happening in Room 109: My students and I were truly working as coresearchers and colleagues in the classroom.

> In classrooms where teachers are conducting classroom research, students too can become inquirers and sometimes collaborators in inquiry. When this happens the classroom changes. Students and teachers form new relationships based on negotiation and trust. Expertise is shared. The focus of a class shifts to include student voices. Students become more responsible for how as well as what they learn. (3)

Today, Room 109 is a place of inquiry. My young colleagues and I use reflection and collaboration as a way to learn and grow. *Reclaiming the Classroom* by Dixie Goswami and Peter Stillman and *The Art of Classroom Inquiry: A Handbook for Teacher-Researchers* by Ruth Shagoury Hubbard and Brenda Miller Power are two books on teacher research that offer wonderful stories as well as the nitty-gritty information for anyone interested in coming to know his or her practice.

Student Reflections

At the end of each nine-week quarter, around the time portfolios come in, I ask my student colleagues to write a first draft expressive piece discussing the class, their work, themselves, and me. At the beginning of the year, I offer a dozen or so primer questions to help them along. By third quarter, they're usually on their own.

Having students reflect on and evaluate a class is not unique; and contrary to what I once thought about in-class research, one doesn't need an incredible amount of time or special training to make meaning out of the comments. Listening and caring are the keys.

For my young colleagues, these reflections offer one more opportunity for their voices to be heard. Because they have seen their comments and ideas change Room 109, they know I take their thoughts seriously. As a result, they write seriously as well.

Most students write from three to fifteen pages of reflections. Even though the combined writings create a book of five hundred to eight hundred pages, it is a quick, fun, and engaging *read*; after all, it's all about what we do together.

As I read, I highlight the interesting lines. I used to think I needed some fancy formula from a teacher-researcher guide to decide what, indeed, was interesting. Finally, I trusted my instincts.

Once read, I select representative quotations and put them into a synthesis. It usually takes me bits and pieces of time over a week to read, highlight, select, and type out the final package. In a way, each quarter-end collection is a chapter in *The Book of Room 109*. Each helps me learn. It is true: "The word for teaching is learning."

By sharing my students' words with one another, they see they are not alone in this venture. All those feelings of frustration, satisfaction, anger, joy, and exhaustion are shared, to one degree or another, by all the workers in class.

I know the students grow from the writing of reflections and the reading of the synthesis. As for me, their words have changed my teaching and, in a very real sense, the person I am.

Here's an example of primer questions for a quarter-end reflection. My students may use these or go off on their own.

My Dear Students,
    It's time for some real fun and some honest to goodness learning. In 109 we call them *Reflections*. (I can hear you cheering!)

Learning experts tell us that "We learn by thinking about what we have done." I'm sure you're thinking, "Okay, Kent. Just tell us what we have to do and be quiet!" Okay. If that's the way you want to be.

A reflection is a chance to look back at what you've done and to think about it on paper. This thinking and writing is a way to learn. A way to come to know. And, my 109 scholars, this is good!

This week while I'm reading and responding to your portfolios is the perfect time for you to write a reflection. First, there's little pressure. Second, what else do you have to do? Third, this needs to be in your second quarter portfolio! This is like a Blue Light Special at Zayre's!

I'll give you a few primer questions, use them if you like. *Please compose this on a computer or word processor and spell check.* Thanks. This reflection does *not* have to be edited, but a spell check is a good way to smooth the thing out. *Again, this is a first draft piece of writing.* Just write what comes into your head and simply get on with it!

1. Why is our theme "balance"?

2. Speaking of Room 109 and your work in here . . . over the last nine weeks what makes you most proud? Explain why this is so.

3. Why do you think I use portfolios?

4. Look through the papers and stories and essays you've written. Which one would make you say, "This is my best." Why is it your best?

5. Speaking of writing . . . how has your writing process changed this past nine weeks? Or has it? Do you use editors? Have you been revising/drafting? How will you change as a writer for the next quarter?

6. And speaking of speaking . . . how are you doing as a communicator? As a listener, a speaker, a performer, a viewer, an observer, and a presenter? Have you added into our class discussions the way you would like?

7. What sort of goals have you mustered up for yourself after this first nine weeks? Do you have any big plans for your work during second quarter? Did you get bitten by the *Procrastination Bug*? How do you judge your performance?

8. Look at the following quotes extracted from reflections at the end of first quarter last year. Speak about one or both of them in relation to your experiences in English.

   Room 109 isn't so much a room, it's a way of thinking, an attitude towards learning, discovering.

   I think that you expect too much from us. We are not perfect. Your expectations are too high.

9. Look back at the projects you produced. What's the one you'd like to hold up and say, "This is my best." How are you going to change the way you do or think about projects in the coming quarter?

10. Explain why you think I believe reflection (e.g., thinking back about what you have done in here) is so important. In the same essay, explain this: *We learn by thinking about what we have done.*

11. Discuss whatever you think I've neglected. Your classmates. Mr. Kent. Whatever comes into your head. Ramble on!

So, that's it. You've survived the first quarter of 109. I hope you feel good and are ready to begin again next week. I hope all of you will find new ways to move your work to the next level.

YLET,
Rich Kent

Here's part of the fifteen-page synthesis that came from the 650 pages of my students' first-quarter reflections. The only sounds I hear while they're reading are a few chuckles and muffled groans. I ask them to highlight those comments they would like to discuss.

(There are times when I don't feel like typing out the synthesis, so I ask each member of each class to come to my notebook computer and type in the line or two that I have highlighted from their reflection. I've also had kids pick their own quotation to include in the synthesis. This hasn't been received well thus far. I try to pick a wide range of comments; students seem to focus on comments that are particularly funny to them and a few select friends. The rest of us simply don't get them.)

My Dear Students,

Your words of reflection ran the gamut, from satisfaction to resignation, from celebration to anger, from impassioned vows to improve to colossal sighs of relief. It is always amazing for me to read my student colleagues' responses to their quarter's work. In many cases reflections include some of the best writing of the year. This group is no exception.

Reading this collection as a whole—as a book of nearly 650 pages—helps me come to know more about teaching and learning. Indeed, it is one of the ways I learn. This reading also gives me insight into you, my students. I believe with all my heart *If a teacher is not listening to his students, they are not listening to him.* And if this is the case, no one is learning much.

Enough. I found the following quotations immensely interesting for many varied reasons. Together, these lines tell the story of a room called 109 and the people who push on its walls each and every day.

In Retrospect

*My mind is the best place I ever visited, and
I plan on stopping there frequently.*

I definitely had fun and I love doing portfolios! Can you believe it? Someone likes them!

My journals this quarter are wrapped around pure emotion.

Yes I was bitten by the procrastination bug.

I don't have any new goals for the second quarter just to pass. I could care whether I pass with a 70 or a 90, as long as I don't have to take this class over.

Writing can give you that privacy of not having to worry about what others think.

I'm afraid to be wrong. (In my writing) I always throw in words like "maybe," "possibly," or "sometimes."

The most vivid events in my memory of room 109 range from announcing my nipple problem . . .

English in Room 109 is a great example of balance.

People don't communicate enough about things that matter.

My best project is my painting—the first one I had ever done.

I liked how you corrected our portfolios by typing us a letter . . . it made all the work not seem that bad because you read it and told us what you liked about it.

Reading has also been a problem. I guess I'm still searching for the right book. I lose my concentration when I'm reading and end up spending many hours on one page. I really wonder if whether I have some sort of learning disability.

When I did my project on Brazilian music I felt that I had so much to share and show.

This portfolio is me and I can look at myself in a different sort of mirror just by reading through my own portfolio.

I'm just getting to the point where not much matters.

I bet you don't procrastinate, Mr. Kent.

It's all about reality and looking between the lines.

Yahoo, this is the best part of Mr. Kent's English class. This is the time when in a ten hundred page essay we get to tell him what a jerk face he is.

To write a reflection, the writer's mind must be open.

I don't have anything else to say, Mr. Kent.

Indeed, different people see life—*and 109*—differently. Is that okay? Absolutely.

You might like to use some of these quotes as the genesis (beginning) of a paper. You might like to stick this collection in the back of your second quarter portfolio under *Kent Stuff*, and simply get on with life (a.k.a. portfolio). Fair enough.

I do hope you appreciate hearing the thoughts of your colleagues. We all have something to say.

YLET,
Rich Kent

PS Next quarter I will have each of you select one quote from your reflection and type it into Little Ralph. It'll be fun to see what you choose for a quotation. I've never done this before; it'll be cool. (NOTE: two independent clauses combined by a semi-colon.)

Looking Closely at Reflections

When I first began assigning and reading reflections, I felt lost. I struggled to create meaning out of my students' words. At times, my stomach felt as if I were driving the back roads of western Maine. Maneuvering Byron Notch can be a wild ride over curvy, potholed logging roads. The end result is a stunning view of Tumbledown Mountain quite like the Matterhorn in the Pennine Alps, but getting there is a chore.

As a novice reader of reflections, I got caught up in reading about "me." In fact, sometimes I would skim right through a reflection to find what they said about their "loving English teacher." Some of the extreme comments left me reeling.

> Dear Mr. Kent . . . As a teacher I don't particularly care for you. I think your class sucks. There is a ridiculously huge amount of work in your class. Most of the stuff we read in your class is junk . . . I'm learning nothing in this class that will help me in any way in my life. I already know how to read and write and unless St. Exupery is going to do my taxes for me I'm not going to learn how to do anything in class that will actually help me in reality.
>
> Dear Mr. Kent . . . I hope you fucking die in a car crash on your way home.
>
> Dear Mr. Kent . . . You are a horrible, untollerable, impatient, anal-retentive, conniving weasel.

Other comments had me convinced that I was, indeed, *a gift* to the teaching profession.

> This class expands your mind and gives you a new way to deal with the every day.
>
> You drove me insane sometimes—I think you expected too much . . . but then if you hadn't, I wouldn't have tried so hard.
>
> Mr. Kent, this class has changed my life.

Now that I've read thousands of pages of student reflection, I've learned to be a more objective observer. I don't ride the waves of individual comments—good or bad—but manage to see the larger picture. (Of course, I don't deserve to die in a car crash because I assigned forty-eight journal entries. And I am convinced no school would survive with an entire staff of Mr. Kents.) Selecting lines from reflections and placing them into a synthesis helps put my practice into perspective. These collections force me to see beyond my role in class.

Since my practice has matured and students are more aware of the expectations here, the comments have become less extreme. This happened because I have learned to introduce the 109 philosophy more skillfully. Also, most kids know the requirements before they walk in the door on the first day. There are times when it's good to have a reputation.

At Bread Loaf/Oxford I wrote reflectively about my students' reflections. Thinking about reflections is one thing; writing about them is another. That summer I selected ten student reflections from the previous year and wrote two hundred pages of analysis. I'd like to say I continue to write these types of studies on a regular basis, but I don't.

Personal letters in response to portfolios and developing a synthesis of reflections help me think about my practice as a whole. This is teacher and classroom research. For any teacher who is experiencing reflections for the first time, writing an analysis would be helpful. How do you do one of these? Just write whatever comes into your head about the student's comments. The more you write, the more you see.

Here are excerpts from some of my first analyses of student reflections:

Kristen readily admits that her writing is positively affected by the conversations we have in class. "If we didn't have the talks," she says, "I know I would not be able to write well." Our discussions serve as both model and catalyst for Kristen's writing and thinking. With the various voices and ideas within the room, Kristen begins to see and to understand (make meaning) out of a subject. It is then that she's able to write more forcefully about it.

Lincoln begins with an easy-going "kinda" writing that is extremely expressive and fun. "I ain't an orderly kinda guy," he admits. One can almost see the twinkle in his eye. "My rooms a mess, my closets trashed, I have three hundred magazines all over the place, the only thing in some kind of order is my baseball card collection."

Yes, Lincoln's grammar is weak, but what he says is not. His writing is rich and honest and full. Using one of my lines in an effort to connect more directly with me, his reader, Lincoln says, "My punctuation in my portfolio is not great. I am not, I repeat I am not good at punctuation. I just write, I mean 'It's not the Olympics,' Right, Mr. Kent?"

It's true, Lincoln "just" writes, but his writing shines. What I hear from Lincoln is the struggle to conform to the institution's rules and regulations concerning writing performance. He speaks about his weak punctuation, his inability to take good notes, and his poor spelling . . . "that word scares me," he admits.

In her final reflection, I see growth in Tania's ability to express herself more freely, more fully, and more honestly. This can be attributed to a number of factors: the amount of expressive writing undertaken, the 135 hours of class time we have spent together, the relationship we have developed both in and out of the classroom, and her growth as a student and a person.

When Ryan writes about the class, he talks about how he is helped by his classmates. The focus is on him as subordinate—in fact, he states three times in two pages that his classmates are always there to help him out when he needs it. In the same paragraph he writes about a couple of friends who are lower ranked students such as he is—then he writes about two high honors students (Dartmouth and Bates) who are willing to help him out. He seems to find solace and balance in the fact that he is not the only one in the class with his weak academic background—of course that's pretty normal—and he seems comfortable with the fact that he can call two of the bright students "friends." I believe that's significant as he builds trust within this classroom culture and as he negotiates his place within it. This surely speaks well of the heterogeneous classroom.

Looking closely at my students' writing and responding with enthusiasm and genuine interest is an act of trust and respect. Gaining this level of curiosity took time, practice, and study.

More than Stories by Thomas Newkirk (1989) is a model of looking at and writing about children's writing. Newkirk's sensitive and far-reaching representation of children's texts helps us see the possibilities when we become respectful observers of our children's work. This same sensitivity is illustrated in *The Lives of Children* by George Dennison (1969), though Dennison's work is focused on learning, not specifically on writing. *Wally's Stories* by Vivian Gussin Paley (1981) also supplies an important way of seeing as she writes, "The first order of reality in the classroom is the student's point of view."

Speaking back from the ages, Tolstoy makes us question the traditional role of teacher and student when he asks, "Should we teach the peasant children to write or should they teach us?" (see *Tolstoy on Education*, Pinch and Armstrong 1982).

The answer, of course, is that hand in hand we learn from one another.

Thinking About Thinking and Reflecting on Reflecting: Metacognition

"Okay, let me get this straight," says Sydney. "You want me to reflect on my reflections?"

"Mr. Kent," says Mark, deadpan, head in hand. "Does this *ever* end?"

I have encouraged my students to look back at their own thinking from reflections and . . . to think about it. Thinking about thinking—metacognition—is a playful, yet scholarly time for 109ers. They tell me that looking this way throughout the year makes them feel like thinkers. Perhaps Ryan said it best:

I am a thinker. I think I could be a philosopher, but I don't want to be one. I am constantly thinking about everything. I think it's fun. I will probably continue to think outside the classroom.

By late in the year they have figured out that this Mr. Kent character is, indeed, interested in their thinking. They also know this playful kind of writing has no boundaries—there are no rights or wrongs.

"Just read over your reflections and then write about what you think about what you thought," I say, straight-faced.

"Who's on first, Mr. Kent?" laughs Cory.

David illustrates the purpose of reflecting on reflections in a paragraph from his essay:

This reflection is probably the most effective of the three so far. This reflection sums up all the reflections and lets me answer and ask some questions that may lead into different thinking.

To me, "different thinking" suggests moving to another level of scholarship. Exciting stuff.

Allycia looks into her past writing and thinking while playing with tomorrow:

It's refreshing to look back and see how my thinking has changed so dramatically. If my thinking over the next three years grows at the same rate it did from first quarter to third quarter, I'll be a genius when I graduate from college.

Michael compares his three quarter-end reflections and writes about each in a general way. This comparing helps him make meaning of his efforts:

The second quarter reflection that I created was more of what I see as an ideal reflection. I let all of my feelings flow from my mind out of my fingertips and eventually to the keyboard of my computer (I don't have a name for it like you do.) I really got into my reflection and I put a lot of thoughts on the paper. Letting feelings loose, that is the key to reflection. I was reflecting with skill and grace almost like my soccer headers, the grunt is exclusive to soccer of course.

Finally, in Matthew's essay, we see the power and possibility of reflecting:

Reflections are a story. You're writing yourself, whether or not you even realize it. When I took the time to look back for this paper, I reread the story of my year. I gained more meaning from reading myself than from anything else I have ever read. Reflections allow us to see what our worlds were like when we first wrote back then.

"*I gained more meaning from reading myself than from anything else I have ever read.*"
Enough said.

The Final Reflection

The Final Reflection of the year includes a listing of the portfolio work the students have produced over thirty-six weeks as well as their thoughts on various aspects of the year in English. These reflections include writing samples from the year. Often, the entire package is thirty to forty pages long.

This reflection takes the place of the students' final examination

A Final Reflection
Room 109

We learn by thinking about what we have done.

NAME _____   CLASS PERIOD _____

PHONE _____   GRADE _____

Directions: Fill in the various sections on these sheets where the
space is provided. When a longer response on separate paper is called
for, please use a computer and spell check. Attach those sheets to the
appropriate page. In the end, you will have "A Final Reflection"
booklet. Any questions? Ask.

Books

List the books you read this year in Room 109. For those books
you didn't finish, just make a note what percent of the book
you actually read.

Look over the books you've read this year and think about
them as you write about the following questions. You have seen
some of these questions before.

a. *What has happened to you as a reader over the past year? (Think back
    to August and how you felt about books and reading.)*

b. *Has your taste in books changed?*

c. *Why do you think you have choices of what to read? Is that important?*

d. *What's the "best book" you've read this year and why?*

e. *Do you think it's important for you to be a reader?*

f. *Why are there no tests over books in here?*

g. *Talk about book projects.*

h. *Explain why researchers say, "We read to learn how to write, and we
    write to learn how to read."*

Figure 9–1. A Final Reflection

Book Projects

Tell about your best book project of the year. What made it the best? How might you improve upon it? (Compose this on a computer.)

Dream Project

If you had all the time you needed—let's say a couple of weeks of class time without other English portfolio stuff—and your only assignment in English was to create a "great" book project, describe that project. Don't go crazy with money. In other words if you had a project on The Doors, don't invite them to play. Be realistic. (Compose this on a computer.)

Outstanding Project of the Year

Think back through the year. Whose project—and I know there were many fine ones—touched you as outstanding? Explain your choice. (If there's more than one you'd like to mention, that's fine.)

Explain what this project did to "bring out" the book or idea. Great projects make a kind of meaning of their own. Talk about what's created in you when you see someone's fantastic work.

Writing . . . Writing . . . and More Writing

Room 109 seems to have gotten the reputation that all we do is write. Indeed, writing is thinking and communicating, grammar and reading. Some of us—many of us in fact—might say that *Writing is life*. (I can hear you now! &%$#*& Careful! Ha!)

List the titles of the papers you've written this year and write a one-line theme or synopsis of the work. (You may write these out in ink below.)

EXAMPLE: TITLE: "You Don't Understand! Men and Women in Communication Wars"

THEME: This paper discusses the various ways men and women do and don't communicate; it

Figure 9–1. Continued

also provided insight by including various interviews with students here at Mountain Valley High School.

Quickly look through all of your formal and informal papers for the year. Select what you consider one of your best papers of the year. Write a letter to your *Keepers* about good writing and why this paper fits that. Use the following as ideas in your letter:

a. *Beginning, middle and ending of the papers: Explain the balance and the development of the overall paper.*

b. *Sentence variety*

c. *Idea development, paragraph development*

d. *Voice: Can you hear yourself in the paper? Explain voice to your* keepers.

e. *Editing: Explain who edited the piece and talk about the revision process you went through.*

Keeper Response

Now, the fun part. Attach the paper to the letter and hand it over to your *keepers*. Have them read the work and then write a comment about it. Include their comments—written on a separate page—in this reflection booklet.

Class Participation

Over the past thirty-six weeks you've had good days and bad days in Room 109 when it comes to your participation. That's life, isn't it? Discuss your very best when it came to being a part of this classroom community over the past year. This includes large and small groups, work with visitors, and work with Mr. Kent.

Themes: Balance, Ethics, Diversity, Boredom

Why themes? More specifically, why do you believe that I find *balance* the most appropriate theme for a year-long class?

How do the other themes work to create a balanced class?

Figure 9–1. Continued

A Base of Expressive Writing

Early on in the year we discussed three types of writing: expressive, transactional and poetic. Why do you feel—after *all* of this writing—that we focused so much on *the expressive?*

Stage 109: Acting and Improvisation

Discuss Stage 109. What might these presentations do for you in the future?

Looking Cosely at Film

For those who watched and responded to *What's Eating Gilbert Grape?* has your idea of viewing a film changed? How so?

Our Loving Fire Trap

There's a purpose in decorating Room 109. There's a purpose in having a mass of student work on display. Talk about the physical characteristics of our room. How do you feel when you come in here? Do you think it's important to have this room decorated in this way?

"Dear Incoming Students . . ."

Write a letter to a student who will take English in Room 109 next year. Yes, you may be funny or dead serious if you want, but at the same time try to give them hints on survival. Perhaps you could explain how you succeeded and why. Definitely use a computer and spell check. Thanks.

Journals!
One Hundred and Ninety-Two

48 x 4 = 192

For most of you 192 is the magic number. It reflects a lot of work, a lot of growth, a lot of thinking, and—of course—a lot of suffering. Page through your journals from the past year and select one that you're proud of. Type it out on the computer and talk about it a bit. What makes you proud of this particular piece? Talk about journals in general.

Figure 9–1. Continued

My Portfolios

Look at all four of your portfolios together. Actually stack them on top of one another. Pick them up. Now, write a reaction to your work. Discuss the hours of work. The best moments, the worst . . . the memories. How do these portfolios reflect the person you are? What about that wicked monster, Mr. Procrastination? (a.k.a. Ms. I'll Do It Tomorrow. Mr. Next Quarter I'll Do Better. Ms. I'll Never Fall Behind Again.)

Discuss your organization. Has it changed? What can you learn or have you learned from your successes and failures in Room 109?

"In Room 109 we are all teachers and we are all learners."

Discuss this quotation by Dan Patterson (MVHS '92) as it relates to you, your work, and your classmates.

"Dear Mr. Kent . . ."

This one is all yours.

Figure 9–1. Continued

for the course; they are given a week to complete the work. Because of the extensive nature of this reflection, the students need all four portfolios for reference.

Student Research Assistants

> *We need to remember that our students* do *think important thoughts, and that they have strategies for researching, imaging, collaborating, theorizing.*
> Ruth Shagoury Hubbard,
> "Enlisting Students as Co-Researchers"
> *Teacher Research*

My college teaching friends often speak warmly about their research assistants. Truthfully, having the luxury of such help made me envious. From exploring various sources to sharing conversation, research assistants help professors look more closely and work more effectively on projects.

I have just begun using selected students as research assistants in my secondary classroom. The results thus far have been exciting. I selected four research assistants to help with two projects. The two high school students and two college students (out on summer holiday) are veteran members of my portfolio classroom; they represent a total of twelve years of Room 109 experience.

The first project involved (1) critiquing the Final Reflection package and (2) writing an observation of student responses to these reflections. I posed a series of questions to three student researchers after supplying them with completed reflections from the previous year. Their instructions were to write observations in a first-draft expressive piece.

The collected observations of Final Reflections by these young researchers helped me think about certain changes I would employ. Brooke, a senior, came up with the idea of having each student look through all of his or her writing for the year (e.g., journals, papers, reflections, etc.) and develop a synthesis using selected lines. Developing this synthesis will help all of my young writers look even more closely at their own thinking and their year's work.

In Matthew's thirteen-page observation, this junior created a balanced perspective through a dialectic approach. In the midst of his writing—exploring what he saw as the positives and the negatives of the Final Reflection—these lines appeared:

> *The beauty of nature is that it is unpredictable. The same rings true for 109. What one person sees might contradict what a classmate sees—that kind of conflict leads to the expanding of ideas and the opening of minds.*

Not only does this line capture the philosophical essence of a portfolio pedagogy, but Matthew's words show us his ability to make meaning and to develop a thoughtful understanding of an organization that he is a part of.

The second project involved the oldest student, a sophomore in college named Lincoln who may become a teacher. While I was away at a conference, he substituted in my classes—an added bonus was that he received a stipend for substituting. During his two days in Room 109, Lincoln interviewed each student about her or his independent study. His observations of their work—he wrote a paragraph on each project and then a five-page summary of general comments—helped me look closely at the way I manage independent studies.

Having someone other than me interview my students helped these young 109 scholars look at their own work in a different light. Because Lincoln took his role so seriously and because he worked so diligently at encouraging my students, some of the young people began to take their projects more seriously as well.

During the penultimate week of school, I used my last two personal leave days (we are allowed three per year) to bring Lincoln into my classroom to assist me with finalizing the two research projects. Once again, he received substitute pay, and I enjoyed the input and the freedom that an assistant offers.

As a public school teacher, I have often felt isolated. A lack of connecting to other staff colleagues because of a lack of in-school time creates that feeling. Using student research assistants not only helps in the reinventing of my classroom through ongoing discussions, but this practice also adds a new dimension to the meaning of collegiality.

Visits by University Folks

One of the most effective yet nerve-wracking ways of coming to know one's teaching practice is to invite a crew of university professors and education students to spend the day questioning, examining, and critiquing.

Every year, around March or April, this happens in Room 109. The first year I did this, I didn't sleep well the night before. I knew the idea had merit, but all the same I didn't want to be told I wasn't doing it right. But, the experience was breathtaking, eye-opening, and rejuvenating—all the things learning can be.

The questions, the conversations, the sincerity, and the laughter make this one of the most interesting and high energy days of the years. It's also a day of soul searching and reflection: a day of "full contact learning" for the teacher.

My students thrive on being the center of attention. They proudly parade their portfolios and projects. They willingly lead their college guests around the school to show off places like the Writing Center and the Poetry Garden. Ultimately, however, everyone finds a corner, settles in, and talks learning. Portfolios take center stage.

I can't think of a better way to spend a school day.

Frequently, we receive notes from our visitors. This one is from Professor Sandy Johnson, *a teacher's teacher*, from the University of Maine at Farmington.

To the Denizens of 109,

Thank you—Thank you—Merci Beaucoup—for the exciting time, for the inquiring minds, the joyful and the serious approaches to learning and for the whole-hearted welcome you gave (and we felt) to your special place, Room 109.

We'll spread the word (and the word is light) throughout our own dialogues with teachers, students, administrators, and university faculty about the island of sanity and beauty and striving and articulate examination of teaching and learning you've created at Mountain Valley High.

May you always protect what you have, as you are in the exciting process of changing who you are. The Cereek playwright, Aristophanes said (in 414 B.C. or thereabouts) that, "The wise learn many things from their foes." The value you assign to what you do in 109, the learning and knowing you share with each other and with visitors is the best answer to those who are frightened about what 109 represents.

I am truly impressed, truly delighted, stimulated and excited by what you all are doing. You need to know how rare and special you are.

—With thanks, love and admiration,
Sandy Johnson

Writing Recommendations: Telling the Stories of My Students

"Hi, Mr. Kent."

"Hey. How are you?"

"Great," says the smiling boy whose face I recognize. "I was wondering if you could write me a recommendation for college? I've read some of yours and they're really good."

"Well, thanks. Now, what's your name?"

It happens around Thanksgiving. An onslaught. An invasion of sorts. They wander into my room or catch me between classes in the hallway. A few call me on the telephone. Some are shy, some are nonchalant, others are full of themselves—or, as I'm fond of saying, they're ready to tear a hole in the sky.

Telling the story of my students has become easier with portfolios and reflections as references. (And no, I don't write recommendations for students I do not know. I will, however, edit their essays.) Indeed, because I live in a small town, many of the students I have known for years. Their parents are my friends. I've been to their homes for Christmas dinner; they have visited me at the lake. We have stood together at weddings, anniversaries, and funerals. We have history.

But some of the kids that I write for I know *only* from Room 109. That means in a year I've read hundreds of pages of their thinking and have worked with them in many settings. Ours has not been a casual relationship.

When requested to write—I average twenty to thirty recommendations a year—I ask students to give me one of their portfolios or to gather up some of their best writings. Next, I go to my files and retrieve their reflections. As I reread their quarter-end writings, I copy down some of their powerful lines. Sometimes synthesizing the students' own words into a recommendation helps tell their story.

When returning the recommendation, I include a personal, handwritten note to the student. I place the document in a fresh, new manila folder; and if the student is in one of my classes, I hand deliver the piece.

Most of the young people sit at their desks and quietly begin to read. For many, this is the first time in their lives that they have read an essay about themselves. There are no As or Bs on this report card.

Two things usually happen. First, small smiles come to their faces as they read. I figure that they have just come to the part that recounts a special time we have shared. Or it could be my rendition of something they have done that was noble or generous or wonderful—an act they thought no one had noticed.

Next, when they have finished, most of them read their pieces again. We can never be told enough about how special we are.

Teacher Evaluation
of
Mark Paulin

Mark and Cory shuffle onto the stage in front of eight hundred people. They're lifelong friends, football heroes, and the nice guys of the school. We are nervous for them. Cory checks the strings of his guitar—Mark clears his throat and bows his head briefly. The formality of graduation can suck the life out of the most seasoned performers. The two tenth grade boys settle in. *Our* hearts are pounding as we watch these neighborhood kids. We want them to be good.

Four minutes later. The song written for their senior friends echoes through the back of the auditorium, through the cafeteria to silence. All eight hundred of us stand as one. Many of us blink away tears. Good? No. *Extraordinary.*

I have been waiting to write this recommendation for the past four years. From the very first day Mark Paulin entered Room 109 at Mountain Valley High School, I knew I would admire this young man, but I never realized to what extent. As a first-year English student he impressed me with his lively personality, his brilliantly expressive writing, and his adventurous spirit. Need someone to act a part in class? Mark's there. Need someone to edit during free periods? Ask Mark. Need someone to speak to elementary kids or to high school students or to parents? Once again, Mark's your man.

Singer and song writer. Captain of the football team. Gas station attendant. Artist. Cook. Student council co-president. Published poet. Senior editor and student director of the Writing Center. Student representative to the district's Curriculum Action Team. Peer helper. Student senator. In truth, Mark Paulin is a modern day Renaissance Man. A young man who is as comfortable writing a poem as he is snagging catches in the end zone on Friday nights.

But there's more. Mark Paulin is a blue collar scholar; he earns his grades through hard work. He is insightful and thoughtful. He loves to question and to ponder and to make meaning. In discussions he is open to a wide variety of ideas and perspectives. He never hesitates to state his opinion, is respectful to others, and will argue his point with a smile. He has the confidence and self-assurance of a young man who will lead. He has the poise and personality of a man who will serve.

As a writer, Mark has a sound and engaging voice. His ideas are developed thoroughly; he loves to dig deep, to reach in all directions to discover. Mark understands the value of writing to learn. His richly expressive journals tell the story of a young man, the son of a paper maker from a small rural town, whose vision goes far beyond our little valley. His songs, short stories, poems, and essays sing of his experiences. He captures his listeners—makes us care.

This caring was never more evident than in his final written reflection of his junior year in English. After working at the Special Olympics as a volunteer, Mark decided to develop an independent study project for English by working in our school's resource room. Here's how he summed up his experience:

"In retrospect, this project has been the most meaningful of my school career. The most important thing I have learned is that you don't have to be in college level courses to be considered intelligent. Everyone has their special place in life."

Because of Mark's writing abilities and his winning personality, I asked him to be a student director of the Writing Center. I have watched him work as a volunteer in our student-staffed center. He is warm, genuine, and nurturing; his students know he cares about them and their work. Frequent compliments, honest dialogs, and thoughtful suggestions are the norm. Because he is a powerful and responsive listener, Mark is a superb teacher.

If I were given the pleasurable task of putting together a college community, Mark would be one of my first picks. Indeed, to whatever school he attends, Mark will bring small town values and laughter. He will always be ready with a song. As a learner, he'll savor ideas and search for new levels of understanding. In any game he plays, you can bet he'll give you his all. Finally, Mark understands the meaning of friendship.

So much of who Mark Paulin is can be reached in a simple conversation. He gives me, the teacher, energy for my vocation. He makes me want to be good at what I do. He has made a difference in my life.

After seventeen years in education, I know how important honest evaluations are. I offer this one uncompromisingly.

> Richard Kent, Teacher
> Mountain Valley High School

Teacher Evaluation
of
Josie Bray

> I have strung ropes from steeple to steeple;
> Garlands from window to window;
> And golden chains from star to star . . .
> And I dance.
>
> Lines
> *Arthur Rimbaud*

The stilled room of 10th and 11th grade English students watched closely as she warmed up. Methodical, thoughtful, *professional,* Josie Bray prepared to celebrate her first love: dance.

Her precise movements, sharp eyes, and graceful presence engaged her young colleagues, most of whom had never before enjoyed a dance performance. With the last pirouette, her classroom colleagues applauded spontaneously while a scattering of "wows" whispered across the room. Once again, Josie Bray had touched us.

Josie lives in the small town of Peru in the western mountains of Maine. Her parents, a physician and an administrator, are committed, socially responsible community people who provide vital modeling for their children. Emily and Paul Bray generously serve many within our community and beyond. For Josie, service to others is and will continue to be a major part of her life's journey.

As Josie's English teacher for two of her four years here at Mountain Valley High School, I have spent hundreds of pleasant hours in this young woman's company. Our personal conversations in class are illuminating. Her deep interest in a variety of subject areas demonstrates her curiosity and her insatiable need to know. Furthermore, having read over 350 pages of her writing, from essays and journals to short stories and poems, I have had the opportunity to look deeply into Josie's thinking. While reading Josie Bray, she captivates me *and* I learn.

During the first quarter of her senior year, Josie developed an independent study focused on women. Her self-selected reading for this eight-week study included *Sounds from the Heart—On Listening to Girls; Growing up Female; Women Who Write; Feminine Plural; Heroines; Reviving Ophelia;* and *How to Make an American Quilt.* These books portray the sophisticated reader Josie is.

Among the papers in her quarter-end portfolio was an insightful essay titled "The Role of Women." The following section of her essay shows us the balance and precision that Josie possesses as a writer.

> In an age of sex symbols and double standards, it can be difficult to be a woman. Our society gives a mixed message to women. On the one hand, we have the capability to be whatever we want. Women are encouraged to work hard. We are told to be independent and that it is no longer a man's world. On the other hand, in middle school we buy magazines showing us how to put on cosmetics correctly, how to get the guy we want, how to lose weight, and what is currently considered to be 'good looking.' Our bodies are treated like objects . . .

Because of her critical thinking skills and engaging writing voice, Josie will shine as a writer in college. She understands the process of revision and thoroughly drafts her work until each piece reaches her discriminating standards. As a volunteer editor in our school's writing center, Josie shares her talent with a variety of students. Because of her personality and helpful, encouraging comments, Josie is one of our most popular editors. The experience of editing her schoolmates' writing has ushered Josie to another level.

Josie's various responses to literature—in the form of artistic projects and oral presentations—enlighten and entertain. She never settles for the ordinary. One such project is an exquisite homemade quilt in celebration of *Life 101*. This stunning representation will always grace the walls of Room 109. Whenever Josie presents, all of us know she will be well prepared and that we will learn.

As a thinker, Josie has a balanced, intelligent perspective. She looks at all sides of issues, thoroughly respects others' opinions, and enjoys a healthy polemic. Though Josie is more animated in small group discussions, her large group persona is emerging as she gains experience. As an active, thoughtful listener, Josie is peerless. Her maturity helps her handle paradox and uncover meaning. Further, *everything* is of interest to this young woman. Indeed, Josie Bray is a scholar.

Josie Bray will add to any college community in wonderful ways. She is a gifted artist and a caring friend. I have spent the last twenty years in the company of high school and college students. Among all of my young colleagues, Josie Bray stands tall for her work ethic, her sensitivity toward others and her intelligence.

Sharing time with people like Josie is the reason I became a teacher, and why I still find the profession enriching. After two decades in education, I understand the need for honest evaluation of candidates. I offer this one with unwavering enthusiasm and absolute faith. Josie Bray will make a difference in our world—indeed, she already has.

Richard Kent, Teacher
Mountain Valley High School

10

A Place of Celebration

A View from the Outside

Chicken casseroles, cherry cobbler, and Kent over easy.

A local men's group invited me to its dinner meeting to speak about my writing life. Within ten minutes of my talk, the focus shifted and the questions began to fly about school reform. It always seems to happen.

"I read about how your students teach at the elementary schools and such," said one soft-spoken retiree.

"That's right. We're attempting to offer a variety of experiences for students so that more of their learning is grounded in real-life activities," I said, sitting down on the bottom step of the small church stage. I knew this would go one way or the other.

"You know," he said shaking his head much as my father used to when I pulled a teenage blunder, "we're spending an awful lot of money on all this running around."

A couple of men nodded.

"Thing is," added another, "most of them can't write."

I sat up straight. "Well, we're giving them lots of opportunities. Kids write hundreds of pages a year in my class."

"Then tell me this. Why can't I read their writing? I mean, I can barely make out any of the words."

"Are you talking about writing or penmanship?" I asked.

"Can't—read—their—writing," he repeated, mouthing the words as if speaking through a plateglass window. "They fill out a job application and I can't read a word of it!"

Most of the heads nodded. The wagons began to circle.

"I'm not all that sure why kids' penmanship is so poor. Maybe it's because most use computers now."

"Computers," spewed the retiree as if he'd bitten into a wormy apple.

"Those *things*," spit out another.

"What if the electricity goes out?"

I paused. Then, speaking softly, said, "Mine has a battery. Listen, think about the early twentieth century when those newfangled, gas-powered tractors came on the scene. Can't you hear the conversations between the older farmers and the new ones?

"What if you run out of gas in that thing, you young whippersnapper?

"What if your horse throws a shoe, you old goat?

"Whether we like it or not, times do change, don't they? Many of you know that far better than I."

When I finished, I sensed something. Looking around the room I saw a glimmer, that spark of understanding. Of course, some of the men were not listening. They didn't learn with some guy in a shirt and tie talking at them. These men needed to be a part of it. They needed to build it. To sing it. To draw it. To talk and argue and even eat over it.

Others—those who sat still and whose minds were retelling the story to themselves—their eyes said it all: I'd connected.

Seasons of Belief

> *The law of chaos is the law of ideas, of improvisations and seasons of belief.*
>
> Wallace Stevens

Kelly runs up the hallway to my door. "The fire guys are here. They're on the ramp!"

We swing into action. Kids leap up on desks and remove the dozen or so decorated T-shirts that hang around the room on the clothesline. Tracy, Stephanie, and Mike carefully fold them. *I Know Why the Caged Bird Sings* and *The Places You'll Go* need special care—they don't fold. Kristin, Sam An, and Heidi move quickly around the room removing mobiles, tearing duct-taped posters off the walls, cramming caps and dresses and dried flowers and *stuff* in file cabinet drawers. Someone stacks the wooden projects behind the couches.

In a few minutes, two smiling fire inspectors wander in. They interrupt my internal debate. *Should I take down the gift from a student on the top of my classroom door*, the sign that reads, "Restricted Area—Rumford Fire Department—Keep out"?

It happens two or three times a year. Most of the school knows, and most of the time we get a warning from a student like Kelly. Other times, Room 109 is *history* and has to come down. The rule is clear: Only twenty percent of the wall space may be covered and nothing can hang from the ceiling. (Fortunately, not one inspector has mentioned Amy and Frank's papier-mâché blue marlin for *The Old Man and the Sea* hanging behind my desk. Some things, I guess, are sacred.)

Needless to say, I don't want anyone to be hurt. I just lose sight of things in the midst of all the celebrating. It is, after all, a place of celebration.

With all of this going on in Room 109, is it chaos? To a degree. The room is filled, but so are the portfolios *and* my kids. It's a pretty good trade-off.

Portfolio classrooms blossom. Students venture off, scurrying around as if on a huge scavenger hunt. They bring back *everything*. This can create problems, but I keep a sense of humor and have befriended Sam, the first-floor custodian.

Where do the kids end up? Just about *everywhere*: from nursing homes to fire stations, college libraries to kindergarten classes, funeral parlors to city streets. And certainly farther along the learning road than I ever took them with one classroom text.

We Americans were wonderfully idealistic in the 1800s when we developed schools to mass educate the citizenry. Now, what we have discovered over the years, what we have *learned about learning* echoes these words: "People learn at different rates and in different ways." We have learned that for the best results you can't package education, you can't standardize it, and you can't institutionalize it.

All of us know that learning is a process of discovery, but our schools, for the most part, are places where students have not been allowed to discover for themselves. Most of the time in American schools our students are <u>told</u>. Why? It's easier.

In school, *telling* eliminates most questioning. If questions are removed, order is maintained. As we know, most institutions thrive on order and control. Managers are happier when noise is at a minimum, when everyone is seated, and when no one's in the halls. Why? It looks good, there are fewer hassles, and it's convenient.

But what about the discoveries that are the by-products of endless questions and argument, of wildly chaotic moments, and of that "orderly disorder" that is becoming the creative force of our world? In terms of rethinking our schools, we must not only accept these moments, but nurture them.

I strive to make our classroom a place of conversation, a place where individual learners matter and where each of their investigations *is* the curriculum. This is the brilliance of portfolios. Trusting and letting go is frightening. Our students aren't used to this kind of treatment, and as former students, neither are we.

In our schools students are rarely asked what they think, and if they are asked, not much comes of it. Most of us know from our own school experience that we were rarely a part of the planning of our own learning. *We didn't have a say.* The sad thing is, most of our students still don't have a say. And how is this preparing our next generation?

Every current book we read, every speech we hear, focuses on learner-centered classrooms. It is our *truth* in education. Yet, it is not our reality. Walk the hallways of our high schools and colleges in America and glance into the classrooms. You'll see exactly what I mean. Oh, it's changing a bit, but we have much to do.

I've heard this same little story several times: If we took a surgeon from 1860 and placed her in an operating room of the twentieth century, she would be absolutely lost. However, if we took a nineteenth-century teacher and placed him in a twentieth century classroom, he'd be right at home.

Why, with all the knowledge out there, have we not realized substantive change? Think of it, we're in the business of discovery and learning, yet schools have remained the same. When I first began public school teaching, I was afraid to go against the model of teaching I was brought up with. All I ever saw, all I ever knew, taught me as a teacher to "stand and deliver," to have *all* the answers, and to set the agenda.

With portfolios, alternative assessment, teacher research, students as learner colleagues, and all the rest that goes along with rethinking our classrooms, certainty disappears. What does this mean in teaching and learning terms? Before my rebirth at Bread Loaf as a teacher-learner, I needed to know exactly what the classroom day would bring. And at the end of the day or the week, I needed to know exactly what my students brought away from our time together. So, I gave a test and came up with a group of numbers to make me feel successful.

Back when I led the class and treated my twenty-five students as one, there were those unplanned moments of freedom when the kids took over. All of us know those moments. They are tantalizing digressions, excursions into uncharted territories led by wonderfully energetic teenagers. My junior high school social studies teacher, Mr. Ridge, called these moments "tangents."

"Now be careful, people. We're getting off on a tangent," he'd say, smiling and loving every second. They were amazing moments for both students and teacher, for they felt dangerous and exciting and were, to be sure, wildly unpredictable.

But when these moments, which I considered diversionary tactics to keep us from continuing with the sacred Lesson Plan, occurred in my own classroom, part of me froze up. *Is this the best use of our time? How can I grade them on this? What if the principal comes in?* They were reasonable questions for a person who had studied in American classrooms for eighteen years. These questions wreaked havoc with me at four in the morning, for I began to know instinctively that those wild moments were some of the *best* learning in Room 109.

I couldn't validate those times back then. But, I've learned. Perhaps this is what this book is about. The story of a teacher who is learning to let go and to trust his students while seeking out and nurturing those electrifying moments of discovery. How does one nurture these moments? Think learning not teaching; think *people* not institution, and this place called school takes on a powerful new meaning.

The Best We Can Do

Mid-January. Portfolio week. Four full days of reading, responding, and assessing so far. Sixty-four portfolios to go. My eyes prickle. Back stiffens.

I page through his journal book and this one catches my eye:

> It is Christmas. Snow covers
> the ground and coats the
> trees. The scent of fur bows
> fill the air. Sled highways
> run down the lawn.
> Snowmen wave to you as you
> drive by. Frozen fingers and
> heavy boots. Parades
> downtown. Santa Claus and

his reindeer, Rudolf. Cards
in the mail and presents
under the tree. The color red.
Blinking lights on the houses.
Vacation. Wrestling.
Suicide.

I call his house.
He drives up. We talk.
A good talk.
"Just a feeling I had that night," he says.
I look into his eyes for a sign.
"Don't worry," he says.
He leaves.
I curl up in a chair, wondering . . . worrying.
Sixty-three portfolios to go. One hundred twenty students. Twelve advisees. Forty-two soccer players . . .
We do the best we can.

Epilogue
He graduates from high school fourteen months later.

Together

It's June thirteenth. School will close for the summer in two days. Portfolios have been read and returned, assessments made. Letters and reflections pour in. The parting moments.

Reading these final letters and reflections is an emotional time. My young colleagues' word gifts reflect the struggles and the learning . . . the moments we've shared here in 109. For the most part, these young people are happy with themselves and their work. Some aren't, but still they've learned.

I ask, "Could you have received a high honors grade in here if you'd wanted to?"

Every student answers "Yes."

"If I had kept organized," says Kathy.

"I needed to revise my papers more," admits Scott.

"Journals . . . if I'd just done them!" laughs Amy.

"Projects," sighs Mike. "I am project challenged."

They have, at the very least, figured out that they are capable and that they can do.

This is a life lesson.

My students have learned, grown, and come to know themselves, their classmates, and a bit more of our world. And so have I. These young people are writers and artists, actors and builders, playwrights and draftspeople, poets and electricians, physicists and cooks, comics and singers, explorers and editors, mapmakers and graphic artists, inventors and readers, biologists and speakers.

During our times we have argued and edited, slept and built, laughed and written, stretched the truth and cooked, pouted and invented, stormed out and read, cajoled and explored, wept and sung, eaten and acted, admitted and discovered—all in this little room . . . together.

My Loving English Teacher,

This year has been cool. I'd like to try and get you for next year. At first I thought what kind of teacher doesn't teach? It's not like you don't teach. I feel that you guide and that's good because everyone needs to be guided. And in our own way we kind of guide you.

I guess I said all I wanted to say. Have a good summer.

"Aren't all summers good?"

YLES,
Laron M.

Works Cited

Allen, Janet. 1995. *It's Never Too Late: Leading Adolescents to Lifelong Literacy.* Portsmouth, NH: Heinemann.

Armstrong, Michael. (1980). *Closely Observed Children: The Diary of a Primary Classroom.* London: Writers and Readers Publishing Cooperative Society.

————. (1992). Conversations at The Bread Loaf School of English. In "The Invention and Discovery of Meaning." Lincoln College, Oxford University.

Atwater, James. 1981. *Better Testing, Better Writing.* A Report to the Ford Foundation.

Atwell, Nancie. 1987. *In the Middle: Writing, Reading, and Learning with Adolescents.* Portsmouth, NH: Boynton/Cook.

Barnes, Douglas. 1988. "Knowledge as Action." In *The Word for Teaching Is Learning: Essays for James Britton,* edited by Martin Lightfoot and Nancy Martin. Portsmouth, NH: Boynton/Cook.

Branscombe, N. Amanda, Goswami, Dixie, and Schwartz, Jeffrey (Eds.). 1992. *Students Teaching, Teachers Learning.* Portsmouth, NH: Boynton/Cook.

Britton, J. 1982. *Prospect and Retrospect: Selected Essays of James Britton.* Edited by Gordon Pradl. London: Heinemann.

————. 1991. Conversations at The Bread Loaf School of English. In "Coming to Know Your Classroom: Stories and Theories." Bread Loaf Mountain Campus, Ripton, VT.

Dennison, George. 1969. *The Lives of Children: The Story of the First Street School.* Reading, MA: Addison-Wesley.

Elbow, Peter. 1986. *Embracing Contraries: Explorations in Learning and Teaching.* New York: Oxford University Press.

————. 1990. *What Is English?* New York: Modern Language Association; Urbana, IL: National Council Teachers of English.

Freisinger, R. 1982. "Respecting the Image: A Transactional View of Language and Cognition." *Iowa English Bulletin* 31: 5–9.

Gardner, Howard. 1983. *Frames of Mind: The Theory of Multiple Intelligences.* New York: Basic Books.

Glazier, Teresa Ferster. 1977. *The Least You Should Know About English: Basic Writing.* New York: Holt.

Goswami, Dixie, and Stillman, Peter (Eds.). 1987. *Reclaiming the Classroom: Teacher Research as an Agency for Change.* Portsmouth, NH: Boynton/Cook.

Hillocks, Jr., George. 1995. *Teaching Writing as Reflective Practice.* New York: Teachers College Press.

Hubbard, Ruth Shagoury. 1996. "Enlisting Students as Co-Researchers." *Teacher Research: The Journal of Classroom Inquiry* vol. 4, no. 1 (Fall): 120–25.

Hubbard, Ruth Shagoury, and Power, Brenda Miller, 1993. *The Art of Classroom Inquiry: A Handbook for Teacher-Researchers.* Portsmouth, NH: Heinemann.

Langer, Judith A., and Applebee, Arthur W. 1986. "Reading and Writing Instruction: Toward a Theory of Teaching and Learning." *Review of Research in Education* 13: 171–94.

Martin, Nancy. 1991. Conversations at The Bread Loaf School of English. In "Coming to Know Your Classroom: Stories and Theories." Bread Loaf Mountain Campus, Ripton, VT.

———. 1983. *Mostly About Writing: Selected Essays.* Portsmouth, NH: Boynton/Cook.

Newkirk, Thomas. 1989. *More than Stories.* Portsmouth, NH: Heinemann.

Pack, Robert 1991. Conversations at The Bread Loaf School of English. In "The Poetry of Robinson, Stevens, and Frost." Bread Loaf Mountain Campus, Ripton, VT.

Paley, Vivian. 1981. *Wally's Stories.* Cambridge, MA: Harvard University Press.

Pinch, Alan, and Armstrong, Michael (Eds.). 1982. *Tolstoy on Education.* London: Athlone Press.

Rief, Linda. 1992. *Seeking Diversity: Language Arts with Adolescents.* Portsmouth, NH: Heinemann.

Romano, Tom. 1987. *Clearning the Way: Working with Teenage Writers.* Portsmouth, NH: Heinemann.

Rosenblatt, Louise. 1978. *The Reader, the Text, the Poem.* Carbondale, IL: Southern Illinois Press.

Sizer, Ted. 1992. *Horace's School.* New York: Houghton Mifflin.

Wilhelm, Jeffrey D. 1997. *"You Gotta BE the Book:" Teaching Engaged and Reflective Reading with Adolescents.* New York: Teachers College Press.

Young and Rubicam Foundation. 1991. *The One Place: A New Role for American Schools.* New York: St. Martin's Press.